LIFE ON AUTOPILOT

of related interest

Hell Yeah Self-Care!
A Trauma-Informed Workbook
Alex Iantaffi and Meg-John Barker
ISBN 978 1 78775 245 0
eISBN 978 1 78775 246 7

Trauma Is Really Strange
Steve Haines
Art by Sophie Standing
ISBN 978 1 84819 293 5
eISBN 978 0 85701 240 1

The CBT Art Workbook for Coping with Depression
Jennifer Guest
ISBN 978 1 78775 096 8
eISBN 978 1 78775 097 5

The Recovery Letters
Addressed to People Experiencing Depression
Edited by James Withey and Olivia Sagan
Afterword by Tom Couser
ISBN 978 1 78592 183 4
eISBN 978 1 78450 460 1

Living at the Speed of Light
Navigating Life with Bipolar Disorder, from Depression
to Mania and Everything in Between
Katie Conibear
Foreword by Calum Harris, Lorraine Gillies and Aditya Sharma
ISBN 978 1 78775 557 4
eISBN 978 1 78775 558 1

Life on Autopilot

A Guide to Living with
Depersonalization Disorder

Joe Perkins

*Foreword by Dr Elaine Hunter
and Professor Anthony David*

Jessica Kingsley Publishers
London and Philadelphia

First published in Great Britain in 2021 by Jessica Kingsley Publishers
An Hachette Company

1

Copyright © Joe Perkins 2021
Foreword copyright © Dr Elaine Hunter and Professor Anthony David 2021

Front cover image: designed by Dooder / Freepik.

*The information contained in this book is not intended to replace the services of trained
medical professionals or to be a substitute for medical advice. You are advised to consult a
doctor on any matters relating to your health, and in particular on any matters that may
require diagnosis or medical attention.*

A CIP catalogue record for this title is available from the British Library and
the Library of Congress

ISBN 978 1 78775 599 4
eISBN 978 1 78775 600 7

Printed and bound in Great Britain by CPI Group

Jessica Kingsley Publishers' policy is to use papers that are natural, renewable
and recyclable products and made from wood grown in sustainable forests.
The logging and manufacturing processes are expected to conform to the
environmental regulations of the country of origin.

Jessica Kingsley Publishers
Carmelite House
50 Victoria Embankment
London EC4Y 0DZ

www.jkp.com

Contents

Acknowledgements

I'd like to extend my heartfelt thanks to everybody involved in the realization of this book: all the clinicians who gave up their time to be interviewed, my fellow sufferers for pointing me in the right directions and bravely sharing their experiences, and Jane Evans and the team at JKP for putting it into black and white. I'd especially like to thank the Unreal crew for their constant support and messages of encouragement every time I was feeling wobbly about it all – a kinder, more understanding group of wonderful people I've never found.

In particular, I'd like to thank my partner, Sophie, for her years of unwavering support and for putting up with me, my parents for not kicking off too much about me still occupying their guest room and testing the foundations with loud guitars, Jane Charlton for all she's done for the cause and the sofa to crash on in Penge(!), Howard Swains for writing the *Guardian* article that has helped so many, dodie for being generally lovely and for raising so much awareness, and Jerry and Gilly of Big Jet TV for keeping me vaguely sane during the locked-down writing process.

Note from the Author

Trigger warning: This book mentions abuse (emotional, verbal, physical and child), alcoholism, anxiety, bullying (including cyber-bullying), car accident, death, depersonalization disorder, depression, drugs and drug use, hallucinations, delusions, intrusive thoughts, hospitalization, loss of a loved one, medical descriptions, obsessive compulsive disorder, pregnancy, schizophrenia, self-harm, suicidal ideation and thoughts, cancer, trauma and post-traumatic stress disorder, and war.

All fellow sufferers interviewed in this book are referred to by their first name only – some have requested to remain anonymous or use a pseudonym. I'm aware that nowadays many people and organizations typically avoid using the term 'sufferers' at all, as in a formal context it might be considered an isolating, dated expression or suggestive of unconscious victimization. (At the Unreal charity, we use 'people of lived experience' to be more neutral and inclusive of carers, parents, etc.) However, in this book I'm usually speaking specifically about individuals who have the condition themselves.

'Patients' doesn't seem an appropriate substitute, as that's a term that implies healthcare – for me to use it might suggest I'm only speaking about those who either have a formal diagnosis or are receiving professional treatment, which isn't the case. Given that living with depersonalization, especially long term, is so debilitating and can have a hugely detrimental impact on all areas of our lives, I've made the value judgement to continue with the term 'sufferers' throughout this book. Whenever it appears, you could substitute it for 'people living with the condition' or 'those experiencing symptoms', if you so wish, but I believe the word 'sufferers' aptly and succinctly describes the distressing experience of depersonalization disorder from the perspective of somebody living with it themselves.

Foreword

Despite the progress that's been made in raising awareness of Depersonalization-Derealization Disorder (DPD), and the increase in information that people can access about DPD, there is an enormous need for a book like this. As anyone with DPD will know, there is still a long way to go to get this condition taken seriously and for there to be enough resources for people who are experiencing DPD to get the help they need and deserve. A book written by someone who has personal experience of DPD and who can explain the current state of knowledge about DPD in an accessible way will be of great benefit to others in the same situation. Joe Perkins has delivered such a book. It is the first of its kind and will perhaps prove to be a landmark for people living with DPD and the field as a whole.

When we first set up the Depersonalisation Research Unit at the Institute of Psychiatry, Psychology and Neuroscience, back in 1999, there was no research in DPD taking place in the UK and very limited awareness of the condition among GPs and mental health professionals. This was despite DPD having been identified as a condition and documented in the psychiatric literature since the late 1800s. The lack of awareness meant that those who experienced DPD had an extremely difficult time getting a diagnosis, let alone treatment. There was a 'Catch 22'-type situation that maintained how difficult it was for anyone with these symptoms. The lack of recognition of the symptoms by professionals led to a lack of DPD being diagnosed. This meant that the widely held belief that this was a very rare condition was maintained. Moreover, this belief in DPD being rare led to a lack of interest and funding for research. And in turn this meant there was a lack of understanding about the condition and very sadly a lack of effective treatments. Luckily, our research unit was started by a generous charitable donation from a family who had experience with DPD and who realized that funding research would be a way of changing this situation.

Over the past 20 years, things have improved considerably, although there is still a long way to go. Our team of psychiatrists, psychologists and researchers at the Depersonalisation Research Unit in the UK, alongside some other groups internationally, such as that led by Dr Simeon in the USA, Dr Michal in Germany and other researchers globally, have helped raise awareness of the condition and carried out various lines of research. In our time as researchers and clinicians, we have spoken to hundreds of people with DPD, which has enabled us to have a much better understanding of the condition.

The use of the internet to access and share information has been of enormous benefit during this period. As Joe describes in the book, many people with DPD only find out that their experiences are a recognized disorder by typing symptoms into search engines. They then must go armed with this information to their clinicians and teach their GPs or mental health professionals about DPD. This situation is improving, but slowly.

However, although there is now more information about mental health, including DPD, online, it can be hard for people to distinguish what is good-quality information from internet sources. Joe decided to use the opportunities the internet provided, particularly YouTube, to make accessible and informative videos about his experiences and to share this with others. I know of many people for whom these have been transformative. Joe has continued to want to help others with DPD and for the past few years has been actively involved with Unreal, the only UK charity specifically for DPD.

Although talking to knowledgeable professionals can be helpful to people with DPD, talking to someone else who has shared this experience offers something irreplaceable. One of the things that's unusual about DPD compared to other mental health problems is that the majority of those who have the condition may never have spoken to another person with the same experience. Speaking to someone who can understand and empathise with your symptoms because they themselves have experienced, or are currently experiencing, the same things is incredibly helpful. This is particularly true with DPD where people experience a sense of intense isolation and disconnection as part of the condition, so making a connection with another is even more valuable.

In this book, Joe describes his own experiences with honesty and openness, interviews other people with DPD to get a broad range of perspectives and speaks to professionals with both clinical and research experience in understanding, assessing and treating people with DPD. This enables him to speak from the heart as well as the head. He also manages to collate all this together in a highly readable and engaging way to inform and guide the reader so that they might have a better understanding of what they are going through, as well as providing some strategies that might provide some relief. He is able to explain sometimes complex concepts in straightforward, non-academic, language.

Joe says at the start of this book that one of his aims in writing this is the hope that people with DPD reading it will feel less alone. We're sure that he will be successful in achieving this. When you read this book, you will feel a sense of recognition with Joe's own difficult experiences, which he explains with a light touch. The reader knows that the writer *really* understands what DPD is like, and his hope to offer guidance and support to others, his warmth and compassion driven by a strong commitment to helping others with DPD, shines through. We're sure you will find it of benefit, and we welcome this unique and helpful addition to the DPD literature.

Dr Elaine Hunter, Consultant Clinical Psychologist
Professor Anthony David, Consultant Neuropsychiatrist

Preface

When I sat down to begin work on this book over Christmas 2019, 'coronavirus' was a word I'd vaguely picked up on in news reports coming out of China, but that was it. I didn't for one minute think my writing would be done in the shadows of a global pandemic, with most of us under 'house arrest' and barely a plane in the sky. If I'd suggested that on Writing Day 1, I'd probably have been ushered deeper into the Maudsley (the renowned psychiatric hospital in London) than the outpatient psychological therapy unit I'd recently been discharged from.

A few weeks later though, Covid-19 had erupted. Hundreds of thousands were losing their lives. Social distancing became the new priority. Our TVs were strewn with webcam footage telling us to come together. Every email sent and received had to make reference to staying safe during these unusual times, and we were suddenly hyper-curious about what our video-conferencing colleagues might be wearing on their bottom half. Jeff Bezos got richer. Toilet roll became currency. Everyone got progressively twitchier about haircuts.

We saw the true colours of politicians buried underneath their wartime rhetoric. My grandma couldn't understand why she wasn't getting her newspaper.

Unusual times indeed.

But for a sufferer of depersonalization disorder, everything felt bizarrely familiar. Suddenly, the whole world was using the same lines I typically resort to in an attempt to communicate what my condition feels like. Everybody was saying, 'It feels like none of this is really happening. It's like being stuck in a horror film. It all feels like a terrible dream.' I'd never want to be facetious and suggest the peak of the pandemic was anything other than a nightmare of global proportions – of course it was. But when trying to describe depersonalization in a way non-sufferers can relate to, the whole scenario has become something of a globally relatable metaphor.

The 'Is-this-really-happening?' nature of it all was nothing new for the likes of me. A few sufferers I spoke to felt the heightened anxiety was affecting their mental health but, on the whole, most said everything was largely business as usual. I didn't see my partner for three months because we were stuck 200 miles apart, and most interviews for this book had to be done online, but otherwise, nothing much really changed in my life. Yes, it all felt like some kind of warped fever dream – but so has everything else for over a decade. I think I've been social distancing for 30 years anyway.

Having the world's worst broadband, talking to everybody over Skype became pretty analogous too. Most people had a great connection: it was stable, with a crystal-clear picture, and conference calls were much the same as real life – only with some slightly wacky backgrounds. Mine was glitchy as hell, the pixelated picture would freeze, half of what was said wouldn't come through, I sounded like a nonsensical Dalek, and the whole routine left me desperate to actually *be* with real people again as I repeatedly wanted to stick my fist through the screen.

So, as you enter into this book, if at any point during Covid-19 you felt disconnected from the reality of what was going down, if it was hard to differentiate news bulletins from fictional thrillers, if having your freedom taken away and being forcibly isolated was tough to deal with or even if Facetime didn't quite feel as satisfying as a 'real' chat with your mates down the pub, then you might already have a sense of what life for a sufferer of depersonalization disorder is like.

1.
Introduction

Head Thing

Several years ago, I found myself walking along a sandy beach in Donegal, a place best summed up by comedian Frankie Boyle as being 'a very beautiful, very bleak part of Ireland' (Boyle 2020). I was with an ex-girlfriend and we'd flown over a few days before for a family wedding. I was having a particularly bad time with the *head thing*: my best attempt to describe the 'spaced-out' feeling I'd had for six years at that point, and which only a handful of people knew about.

No medical professional had been able to offer any clue as to what it was or what might have been causing it. 'Sounds like anxiety – it'll pass,' one doctor shrugged. 'It's probably nothing,' another told me as they stood up and showed me the door after I'd pleaded with them on the verge of tears for ten minutes. A psychiatrist once spent two hours scribbling down my life story, only to prescribe me Prozac without wanting to tell me why. 'Just try it.' At 3am a few weeks later, I suddenly became aware that I was pacing around my shared student house in just my pants, hugging a giant box of cornflakes and feeling like my brain was electrocuting me. And so I returned to the psychiatrist and asked to try something different. But having turned down the alternative offer of anti-psychotic drugs, I was immediately discharged from the service with no discussion or ongoing support. 'There's nothing else we can do for you.' Back to square one.

Anyway, I've never been one to participate willingly in mindless small talk, and whenever I'm struggling to deal with my overwhelming sense of unreality, I need my own space more than anything else. As a stubborn introvert, being forced to exchange pleasantries with people I barely know is draining enough at the best of times. So, walking along that beach with the numerous members of my ex's extended family, I chose to stay slightly away from the main group – trying to gather my thoughts and relate in any small way I could to the grey, overcast views of the sea and rolling hills that didn't feel like they were really there.

For a group of people strongly bonded by their traditional family values, it turned out this was something of a social faux pas. I found out later that a family member had remarked, 'Just *look* at him. What's wrong with him?' and this was later offered up as evidence by my ex during one of our rows about my lack of positivity, which defined the breakdown of that relationship. The head thing was crippling my abilities to relate to the outside world and function as an emotionally present human being. Acting my way through the disconnection and pretending I was fine was becoming harder by the day. In truth, I'd have had no good answer for my ex's relative had they asked me directly. I didn't know what was wrong with me and neither did anybody else. I was fading away, my sense of reality was slowly dripping through my fingers and I was feeling ever more hopeless as things deteriorated.

I know this sounds overly dramatic, but unless you've experienced it yourself, the only thing more terrifying than having a health problem take over your body is going through that process not knowing what the problem actually is. There are so many unanswered questions. 'Am I going to die?' 'Have I gone loopy?' 'Have I got a brain tumour?' 'Is someone drugging me?' 'Will I be sectioned?' 'Am I schizophrenic?' 'Will this ever stop?' A mystery illness progressively steamrolling chunks of your life is a harrowing experience.

I now know that I'm suffering with depersonalization disorder ('DPD' – more about this acronym shortly), but that diagnosis didn't come about until after I'd discovered the term myself in a *Guardian* online newspaper article (more about this in Chapter 2). After years of late-night sessions on Google, trying desperately to apply symptoms of bizarre conditions to myself, as soon as I found that website, I *knew* my problems couldn't be anything else. The symptoms fit like shrink-wrap.

Slowly, I began to build up a picture of what might be going on in my head. It wasn't easy to take it all in, especially given how vacant I was feeling, but any information was precious. I swotted up, printed out paperwork, emailed the journo who'd written the article and was put in touch with the piece's main case study (more about the gem that is Jane Charlton later on). Finally, I approached a doctor and asked to be referred to the Depersonalisation Disorder Service at the Maudsley Hospital. There was much eye-rolling and most of the paperwork was handed straight back to me, but eventually they agreed to pass the Maudsley referral details on to their practice secretary – after telling me all the reasons why I wouldn't ever get there.

In total, it took ten years from the first onset of my symptoms to getting an official diagnosis at the Maudsley in 2018. But I'm far from being alone in that – the average diagnosis period here in the UK is 7–12 years (Hunter, Charlton and David 2017). That's a painfully long time to be feeling like you're losing your mind and cuddling cornflakes in your underpants.

So, why is some scruffy-haired guitarist, still living with his parents in his thirties, putting pen to paper about his battles with mental illness? After all the years of seeking support and trying every conceivable approach to help myself, I haven't yet been able to stop the symptoms from worsening over time – let alone have them improve. So how are my ramblings relevant?

The frustrating truth is that despite being very common, DPD is still all but unknown – not just in general society, but in medical circles too. Since reading the *Guardian* newspaper article, out of all the professionals I've spoken to and had treatment sessions with, I can count on just a couple of fingers the ones who'd even heard of the word 'depersonalization'. Everybody knows about obsessive compulsive disorder (OCD) and schizophrenia, and we all have an idea about how those conditions might manifest themselves in a person, even if they're just vague assumptions. So how is it that DPD is still such a mystery? It's just as common as those other two conditions – all three are believed to affect 1–2 per cent of the global adult population (Hunter, Sierra and David 2004). In addition, many of the eventual DPD diagnoses only come about once the struggling individual discovers the condition themselves and 'pitches' it to the experts. That's surely the wrong way around.

This book sets out to address these issues. Getting my head around the science behind the disorder has been very important for me – a basic understanding of what's going on in my head has taken away some of the mystery factor and made the horrible sensations that tiny bit more bearable to live with. I'm going to be speaking with leading experts from around the world to help explain what DPD is from a clinical standpoint, and how it's treated.

But in addition to the medical nitty-gritty, I have over a decade's real-world experience of living with DPD and dealing with everything that's come along with it: from the early years of it being the head thing to discovering the condition for the first time; navigating the health services and fighting to get to where *I* know I need to be; having friends tell me they want nothing more to do with me because of my problems; trying to describe what depersonalization feels like to my family in vague metaphors; having romantic relationships implode; pushing to stay productive and motivated despite everything feeling meaningless; working at jobs; not working at jobs; adjusting my core beliefs on what constitutes 'success' in this world. None of it has been easy – and absolutely still isn't – but those are all problems that'll ring true for any fellow-sufferer. I hope this book might help us all feel less alone than I have until recently.

Let's quickly clear up a common area of confusion. There's a lot of jargon surrounding the condition, which is made even more complicated by the fact that there are similar words for similar things, which we then abbreviate in inconsistent ways. I'll be explaining what all these mean in later chapters, but here are some of the most widely used terms and acronyms you might encounter:

- depersonalization (DP)
- derealization (DR)
- depersonalization and/or derealization (DP/DR)
- depersonalization disorder (DPD)
- depersonalization/derealization disorder (DPRD or DDD or DPDR or DRD)
- depersonalization–derealization syndrome (DDS)
- depersonalization and feelings of unreality (DPAFU).

There are a couple of important differentiations to be made in that lot, both of which will be discussed soon (namely, the difference between DP and DR, and then between them being either transient symptoms or a chronic disorder). But those two things aside, most of the acronyms are very often used by sufferers as quasi-interchangeable terms – they do refer to subtly different things, but up to a point, we have a tendency to use any of them to get our point across. Technically, I experience both depersonalization and derealization together as a chronic disorder, so DPRD would be the 'correct' term for me to use – but for the purposes of this book, I'll stick with DPD. It's more commonly used, it rolls off the tongue better, it's how I branded my YouTube channel (*DPD Diaries*) and, frankly, you know what I mean. I think the thing that matters is consistency of use.

For me, dealing with the day-to-day ramifications of living with a mental health problem has been just as important as seeking medical treatment and understanding the psychology behind it. I'm going to be combining all of these worlds by explaining what DPD is (with the help of some medical friends), discussing my own experiences and the things that have helped me make it this far, and also looking at some areas of modern life that I believe can degrade our mental health if we sink too deeply into them.

2.
Brief History of Your Author

Don't worry – I'll keep this chapter as short as I can. I'm definitely not interesting enough for this to be any sort of memoir. But, as I hope you'll see later, there are factors about my life and upbringing that tie in strongly with the medical theories surrounding DPD. I'm also very aware this might read like a bit of a pity party. I honestly don't mean it to, but with childhood adversity being so common in this condition, I think discussing mine is important for context. I'll be discussing some difficult life experiences here, so if you're not in the right headspace to shoulder somebody else's baggage right now, please feel free to skip to one of the more support-related subsequent chapters.

I was born in the 1980s (although only by two weeks) in Bristol, in the South West of England, where I still live today. In many ways my early childhood was fairly normal, but even as a toddler my mother noticed I never had much interest in interacting with other kids – I usually preferred to be off doing my own thing. I also had some slightly bizarre interests: first it was washing machines, then carwashes (as in, the big brushy ones at petrol stations). I think it was just a fascination with the spinning mechanics, but not your typical childhood obsessions. A love of aeroplanes followed, which has never gone away – I love the physics and procedures of flight and, if I ever overcome depersonalization, retraining as a commercial pilot is something I'd love to do.

My family was keen to give me the best education they could, which involved me being sent to a nearby private school that looked just like Harry Potter's Hogwarts. It was chosen with the best of intentions, but holy hell, I did not fit in there. From day one I was a sitting duck for the bullies and was very quickly singled out as an easy target – something that would haunt me for the next 13 years (and, as we'll see later, still does).

Every morning, the same group of kids would collaborate on a story about something I'd supposedly done, then run to one particular teaching assistant, who would always believe them. No matter how outlandish or ridiculous, the rule of 'many trumps one' was drilled into me from the get-go as the gullible staff would bellow at me on a daily basis for things I didn't understand. Once, the bullies tied my coat (with me still in it) to a fence and said I'd done it to avoid lessons. Another time, I'd supposedly hurdled over the school gate and was lying down in the middle of the road. Whatever fiction they dreamt up, I'd done it, no questions asked.

Things got really bad around the age of eight. Having moved from the junior school into the middle one, the bullying got much worse, and the staff charged with sorting it out were fighting a losing battle at best. In 2011 I wrote a song about this period for my first album. It began: 'Another day, as others play, sat on my step of stone.' This wasn't poetic licence. I'd found a tiny alcove with a small stone step in it and I would hide there during break times to escape the bullies. It was inconspicuous enough that people would walk past without giving it a second glance, and I generally had pretty good luck making myself disappear there.

One small positive was that in order to escape everything I would throw myself into my schoolwork. With all the studying it turned out I was fairly bright, and after an intense year where the school tried to turn us against each other like some kind of tribute to the Stanford prison experiment ('The person next to you is your worst enemy. You are competing for *money!*'), I was awarded a scholarship to the senior school. I remember that day because my grandparents came over for a celebratory Chinese takeaway in the evening and my grandad brought a bottle of champagne – that was one of the only times I actually remember feeling good about myself.

Another important discovery from this time was my love of music. I'd had piano lessons for years – and hated them – so eventually the teacher gave up forcing me to read classical sheet music and just taught me ABBA songs instead, which I found far more pleasing. Around the age of 13, I started listening to rock music and took my mother's advice to try playing the electric guitar. I instantly bonded with the thing and quit piano lessons that same week. From then on, I spent as much time as I could in the music department, teaching myself Muse riffs, and fairly quickly became good enough on the instrument to perform in school concerts. I always remember the time when some bullies were starting on me, and a kid – who had previously been one of the bullies – barked at them, 'Oi! You leave him alone – he can play "Sweet Child"!' That was my first taste of music potentially being my saving grace in life.

Moving into the senior school, it was hard to imagine things getting worse. However, that place was a savage bear pit of conservative public-school stereotypes. Kids wouldn't bunk off school to get cigarettes. They'd sneak out to the delicatessen to buy smoked meat and foreign cheese. Arguments would erupt over whose daddy earned the most. Somebody's first car at 17 was a pristine classic MG. I'd frequently be labelled a 'filthy commoner'. I know this all sounds painfully clichéd and cartoonish, but it's genuinely how things were – pompous and elitist to the point of vulgarity. You were expected to conform, and if you didn't...trouble.

Having winged the scholarship, I was lumped in with the academics, who already hated me, so there wasn't much competition for the role of punch bag. Property would be vandalized, my gym kit urinated on, guitar strings cut. I'd be clobbered around the head and threatened by strangers. It wasn't uncommon for me to walk into a room and have every person there – many of whom I didn't know – get up and leave in a super-obvious, 'Oh shit, it's *him!*' fashion. Break times would typically be me in one room and everybody else in another, with the door barricaded with a chair. I was left in absolutely no doubt that I didn't belong.

Things became really dark on the handful of occasions where I had kids encouraging me to kill myself. 'Go on, do it!' they'd sneer. 'Everyone hates you... Make the world a better place.' I also remember when 'DIE' was scrawled on my wooden locker – with somebody adding a 'T' on the end a few days later. As a fat kid, I'm not sure which hurt more.

It'll probably come as no surprise to hear that I'd frequently be crying in my bedroom before going to school. I'd often have diarrhoea, and my self-esteem was destroyed. I'd shuffle around looking at the floor, trying to avoid eye contact and constantly feel on red alert, anticipating the next bout of nastiness. Until I was about 14, I can honestly say I had no friends at all. Eventually, I did find a few people I could eat lunch with and hang out with during break times. The bullying continued, but I had that small group who I felt accepted by, which was a welcome change.

My obsession with music only grew stronger as the years went by. There weren't many opportunities for me to get on a stage and play, but once a year a guitar teacher would host a 'band night' in the campus theatre, which would give me a chance to plug in and hurt some ears. One of the real standout moments for me at school was when, after one of those shows, I was walking down the street and a girl stopped me.

'Hey, are you the guitarist from last night?'

'Er, yeah?'

'Well done, you were amazing!'

That's probably a compliment that would make anybody feel good about themselves but, for me, it was so much more than that. I've no idea who that girl was, and she's possibly still wondering why I turned the colour of a beetroot, but she's responsible for a significant moment in my life: somebody actually made me feel...*good*. That was the moment I decided I needed to pursue a career in music.

But here's the irony: it was almost exactly at that point – February 2008 – that I began to feel...odd. My life was starting to look like I'd found some direction and could soon escape to a healthier environment to study something I actually liked. But my brain had a different plan.

In hindsight, I suppose there was a lot going on back then. I chose to sit four full A-Levels, so the workload was massive. I had to record two big pieces for my Music finals but got the 'flu right as I needed to track them, so for a week I was off my face on painkillers, working 18-hour days and wanting to collapse. The bullying was especially brutal. I was exercising obsessively, which added to my fatigue. Plus, it was also the time I consumed a large quantity of cannabis one night (more on this in Chapter 6). But *something* happened that triggered a change in my mind. The next chapter will discuss the sensations in more detail, but for now, let's say I felt a bit hazy – nothing major at first, I just thought I was exhausted.

I wanted to take a year out after school, so I took a job in a high-street record shop at the local shopping mall. It was a great first job in many ways because the people were all lovely and I spent my days surrounded by new music. During the six months I was there though, the haziness became noticeably worse. I'd stand behind the till, looking down the length of the shop and just feel...not there, like I was still asleep and dreaming. By the time I was due to head off to university, I was getting very worried about the symptoms and seriously doubting my ability to get through the course. That was when I first approached the doctor, who said it sounded like anxiety but eventually put me in for MRI and EEG scans (both showing nothing sinister).

Instead of a campus university, I went to a small music college on the Isle of Wight (a tiny island off the south coast of England). The first year was the typical student experience – occasionally we'd sober up enough to actually do some work. I didn't struggle as much as I thought I would moving away from home. With the symptoms continuing to worsen though, it was a real slog to make it through. I enjoyed living with the people I was with and made some lifelong friends, but by June I was quite glad to escape during the holidays for a few months.

In my second year, I struggled a whole lot more. I lived with my mate Josh in a small ex-holiday villa that was pretty grim. There was no insulation or central heating, my bedroom was half underground and stank, the hot water tank only allowed baths an inch deep and we lived next door to the neighbourhood drug dealer. But it served a purpose – we had some good times there.

In the background though, I was falling apart. I wasn't enjoying the course, I felt isolated living on an island and having to pay ridiculous ferry fares to visit home, I was freaking out over how badly spaced-out I was becoming, and as a result I became very depressed. It was during this year that I first began to drink far more than I should have. I'm not sure I'd have been classed as an alcoholic *per se*, and the student musician's lifestyle certainly didn't discourage it, but drinking did become the only way I could cope. Alcohol would make the mental floatiness worse but it 'switched off' the distress. When I was drunk, I knew *why* I was feeling squiffy; day to day I didn't. I'd frequently stop at the local shop on the way home from lectures, buy some cans of whatever was going cheap, then lie in bed and drink it all. Sometimes I'd drink so much I'd go out clubbing on my own, buy some greasy food on the way back, go to eat it in bed, then pass out on top of it.

Josh once jokingly told me the big question at university was always working out which takeaway I'd slept with the night before. I never told him too much about what was going on with me back then – he knew I was going to 'sessions' but not what for. I didn't really know myself, so just didn't have the vocabulary to explain it. He knows the full story now, but I feel bad for being so aloof about it when we lived together, even though it couldn't really be avoided.

I wanted to quit college after my second year but was talked into completing the degree. I'm glad I did, because I enjoyed the final year a lot more. I was in six bands, we played some crazy shows over in Holland and I recorded my first album. Plus, although my alcohol intake was still high, I was able to rein it in and mostly quit drinking alone.

After graduating, I moved back to Bristol and needed a job, so I started working 5am shifts baking bread in the local supermarket. During this time, I met a nice girl and we moved to Oxford later that year. Again, I found myself working in a record shop. Things quickly fell apart though. After just a couple of months we realized we weren't right for each other. The ever-worsening head thing was badly affecting our relationship and, with me often working 13-day fortnights, we never got to spend enough time together to figure out any of the issues. We made it to the end of our one-year accommodation lease, went on a couple of awkward trips around Europe that we'd regrettably booked during happier times and then broke up immediately after.

Moving back in with my parents yet again, I'd reached my wits' end with the symptoms. I'd nearly walked out of the Oxford job many times because I couldn't cope, so I knew another 9-to-5 was out of the question. I kept myself busy making another album but was obsessively spending the evenings scouring the internet and reading up on any condition I thought there was any chance I might have.

But everything changed one night in December 2016 when I came across that online *Guardian* newspaper article entitled 'Depersonalisation Disorder: the condition you've never heard of that affects millions'. What on earth was depersonalization? I had indeed never heard of it. I read on: DPD is 'life lived as an automaton or on autopilot ... an absence of emotions ... limbs are no longer their own ... a zombie-like state ... [sufferers] often do not appear at all unwell ... despite experiencing a total lack of empathy' (Swains 2015).

This freaked me out. It was me. Somebody had literally written this about *me*. After years of trying to convince myself I had everything from heavy metal poisoning to auto-brewery syndrome (genuinely a thing – I bought a breathalyzer), I'd finally found a list of symptoms that was practically bespoke. It *had* to be what I had – there was zero doubt. I emailed the journalist and asked whether he could put me in touch with the lady from the article – Jane Charlton.

He passed on my details and the following day I was invited to give her a call.

What followed was an hour-long conversation that was one of the most comforting chats I've had in all my life. It was my first experience of talking to somebody – anybody – who actually understood. I didn't need to describe the symptoms – she already knew. I didn't need to tell her that doctors hadn't been able to diagnose me. That wasn't just *my* experience. It was *the* experience. For the first time in almost ten years, I didn't feel alone in the struggles. I felt believed. It was like being allowed to blurt out a huge secret after years of keeping it bottled up. I wanted to give her a big hug.

I'll leave the remainder of this story (2017 until the present day) for the subsequent chapters, as the last few years have almost entirely been spent navigating the health services, sitting in therapists' offices and tearing my hair out over the bureaucracy that comes with it all. But I think this is a good place to end for now: I finally had a name for my head thing.

3.
'As If'

The Depersonalization Experience

Let's begin to frame the *haziness* I've been talking about up to now and explain a little more about what depersonalization is like to experience. This is no small task, seeing as it's all notoriously difficult to verbalize.

As mentioned earlier, the first differentiation to make is between the sensations of depersonalization and derealization. They are different but the two are generally comorbid: sufferers experiencing one identify with the other in 73 per cent of circumstances (Baker *et al.* 2003).

Simply put, depersonalization is the fundamental sense that you, as a human being, aren't real. It's often described as a 'loss of the sense of self' (National Organization for Rare Disorders 2007) – the feeling that you're not existing as a conscious physical entity and are detached from the human experience. Derealization, on the other hand, refers to the world around you – *other things* – not seeming real. Looking at your bedroom, for example, and having it feel like a surreal hologram, even though you've woken up there every morning for years. It's like a permanent sense of *jamais vu* (things you know to be familiar seeming alien).

They're both intrinsically similar forms of mental dissociation – the posh medical term for 'feeling disconnected from yourself and the world around you' (Mind 2019) – but depersonalization is first person, as it were, whereas derealization is third. They're a package deal for most of us, so if I ever refer to *just* my depersonalization, I'm meaning the two together. (Again, sufferers tend to use the acronyms somewhat interchangeably, and 'DP' is often our favoured catch-all term for just about everything.)

Secondly, we need to differentiate between these being either transient symptoms or a chronic disorder. As we'll discover shortly, this mental detachment is a clever mechanism of the mind to help us deal with difficult situations, so it *can* be a completely normal thing to experience in extraordinary circumstances. However, it becomes problematic when it starts to be triggered too often as a symptom of other underlying problems – when anxiety flares up, for example, depersonalization might come along with it. There's a correlation between the intensity of both: managing the primary issue reduces the symptom of depersonalization in turn. This is what is meant by 'transient': it comes and goes within a fairly short period of time – usually a few minutes to a couple of weeks.

However, depersonalization can also be ever-present, and this is when it becomes its own standalone, chronic disorder. The sensations last significantly longer: months, years or more. It's believed that the underlying causes of DPD are typically far more ingrained in who we are as a person – the effects of having experienced emotional adversity (especially during childhood), having suffered trauma, the holding of negative self-beliefs, tendencies towards existential thinking – and they typically require professional treatment to slowly reduce the severity and impact of the condition over time. Depersonalization in this instance is the *primary diagnosis* rather than it being a symptom of something else, and it has a nasty habit of not wanting to leave town.

To make this a little easier to follow, from here on I'll use the word 'depersonalization' to refer to the sensations, and the acronym 'DPD' for the disorder (also occasionally known as 'depersonalization syndrome' – they're fundamentally the same thing). Also remember that in the UK, depersonalization is more commonly spelled with an 'S' rather than a 'Z', which is important to keep in mind when searching for texts from different territories online.

The experience of depersonalization is remarkably tough to describe – especially in ways that make sense to the other people in our lives. DPD is often referred to as the '*as if* disorder' because we're so reliant on metaphors to convey what we go through to the outside world. Over the years, the best analogy I've found that most non-sufferers are able to relate to is a state of permanent inebriation. I'll quite often say, 'It feels like being drunk all the time' (to which the reply is usually, 'That sounds great!' I do wish people would stop saying that).

The scenario I try to depict is one of being out boozing on a weekend. You've been at it for hours and you're ten pints worse off. It's about the time of night you find people draped over each other in doorways and start thinking about cheap kebabs. You're sat with your friends in a busy bar. You look around: the place is bustling and noisy and there's loads happening, but because you're drunk it feels almost as if the other people aren't really there and like you're not really there either. It's as though you're floating above the situation. The whole experience doesn't *feel* like it's really happening and you're aware you're probably not going to remember the present moment the following morning. A friend says something, and you reply, seemingly without conscious thought. Words just 'appear' in your mouth. You're not sure how you're making sense. You stagger to the bathroom and knock into somebody. They bark something at you, but the words go in one ear and out the other. You're numbed to the reality. It's like you're stuck behind a metaphorical pane of glass – there's an invisible barrier between you and the things you logically know you should be feeling.

The following morning, thinking back to the bar feels fake. It's like you imagined it, or at least it's not something you were personally involved in. You piece together fragments of memories to fill in the gaps. There are photos on your phone you don't remember taking. It's like remembering a film you saw years ago. You can picture the layout of the building, recall certain events and things that were said, but they're not 'your' memories. You feel detached from them.

Many people can relate to having been out with their mates and having had a few too many drinks at one point or another, although perhaps not to the extent I have (during the height of my drinking I once stupidly downed a pint of what came out of a drip tray underneath some bar taps). Being permanently trapped in that scenario is a pretty accurate portrayal of what depersonalization feels like – just without the slowed reactions. It's the sense that the overwhelming majority of your current situation isn't being internalized – it's not something 'you' are really experiencing or that your conscious mind is registering. Logically, you know the images coming through your eyes are real, but there's nothing about the dulled interpretation of them that confirms that logic to you. You feel like a ghost. Things pass through you.

If you ever hear a former drug addict speak about their experiences (ageing rock stars, for example) they'll quite often say things like 'We feel like we lost the 1980s'. Having experienced DPD for the entirety of my twenties, this certainly rings true for me – that decade feels like it never existed. I can remember things, but they seem so distant and otherworldly. Those years just...happened. Now they're gone. I didn't consciously experience them much in the moment, and my retrospective connection to them – and the years beforehand – is crippled even more by the ongoing dissociation. I've just turned 30... so I'm told. 'Big birthdays' have become reflective landmarks I'd rather not engage with.

Many of us use the term 'autopilot' – you'll remember this was a word that appeared in the famous *Guardian* newspaper article (Swains 2015) – which is a fairly apt summary of the whole experience. I don't want to say 'possessed' because of other connotations that word has, but it's the feeling you're being controlled by something other than your conscious mind or following a pre-determined series of actions. Walking down the road, your legs are going one in front of the other, but you're not *telling* them to. You see an obstacle ahead but before you've begun to think of a solution, you've already side-stepped it. You're acting purely on base-level instinct, like a computer's BIOS. There's a disconnection between your 'self' and your actions.

Another useful parallel is the feeling of waking up first thing in the morning. In 2018 I used this in a short film I made for YouTube (called *Unreal: Life with Depersonalisation Disorder*) and many have since told me it was particularly poignant. Imagine you're fast asleep in your bed and having a vivid dream. The events seem very real to you. In that moment, they are your 'reality'. But then, your alarm clock goes off and you have that strange split second where the two realities blur together somewhat as you transition from the dream into real life. You might find the sound of the alarm briefly manifests itself in the dream as a telephone ringing, or something like that, before you begin to register the *actual* source and become conscious of waking up in bed. Life with DPD is like existing only within that split second where the two realities are crossing over and you're not sure what's a dream and what isn't. I feel like at any moment I could abruptly wake up in bed and find this chunk of my life to have been a figment of my imagination.

In fact, this is more than just an analogy for me – it's a genuine problem that has gotten worse over time. I now frequently find myself struggling to differentiate between real-life events and things I've dreamt. I remember one particular time I was wracking my brain trying to remember something: I'd been to see one of my favourite bands (The Darkness, if that's of interest) in a venue I just couldn't place. Where the hell was it? I could remember queueing outside, the songs they'd played and what the stage looked like. But I just couldn't remember where it was, or when. The Astoria in London? The Waterfront in Norwich? After several months trying to piece it all together, I finally figured out I'd dreamt it. I've seen that band about 15 times, so my brain had plenty of material to draw on to create a realistic depiction of one of their shows. But for months, that dream was 'reality' for me. Or, more accurately, my reality was as dreamlike as the dream was – so everything got swirled in together. I was convinced it'd happened, and realizing it hadn't was a distressing experience.

In Italy a couple of years back, I came across something else that served as a good metaphor, and going through it was far more disconcerting than exciting. In an aquarium in Genoa I put on a virtual reality (VR) headset, and the sensation of seeing things through it was eerily close to my experience of real life. The visuals were, of course, a simulation, but as I moved my head and rotated my body in the swivel chair, the synthesized images reacted to my exact movements. I was swimming with lobsters and getting eaten by a shark, so the events were fantastical enough that I could still recognize they weren't real, but had the VR been showing images of doing the food shopping, it would have been far too close to home. The feeling of being in a vivid, interactive first-person experience that I knew for a fact was make-believe didn't feel all that different from then removing the headset and wandering off to look at a *polpo* (octopus). Life feels like being conscious of existing within *The Matrix*.

There's one more element that I don't really need a metaphor to get across (phew) but this isn't something everybody experiences. I don't have an exact percentage – it seems nobody has ever researched it specifically – but more than the unreality and detachment I've spoken about so far, this is the thing I personally struggle with more than anything else. For some, DPD can cause hyper-emotionality, but by contrast many of us become emotionally numb. It sounds embarrassingly melodramatic to say that I cannot remember the last time I felt happiness, but that's the honest truth of it. The blunting of emotions is something that takes all meaning out of life. How can you, depersonalized or not, have a connection to anything at all if you cannot *feel* it?

You could tell me the most exciting news in the world, or you could tell me the worst, and in response to both I would feel exactly the same: flat. Therapists have helped me to see that the way I used to describe this – 'I don't feel emotions' – isn't strictly accurate, because I do sometimes feel depressed or angry. But overall, my emotional responses are very suppressed, although it seems the negatives are better able to 'break through' the depersonalization than the positives. Perhaps they're stronger and I'm just a miserable git?! But one oddity is that I still exhibit the positive emotions, even though I'd say I'm not feeling them. When a friend walks into a room,

I smile. When a comedian tells a joke, I laugh. But I'm not feeling the elation. Again, there's the invisible barrier. It's like the emotions are *theoretical* – understood, but not felt. The fact I outwardly show them does give me hope that they're still rattling about in there somewhere, and one day I might be able to reconnect with them on a conscious level. As singer–songwriter and YouTube personality dodie describes it:

> Sometimes I feel so numb. I know I feel bad - it's stuck in there somewhere - but I'm just so out of it that I don't know what I'm feeling or where it's coming from.

Those are some of the best abstract descriptions to explain what DPD feels like to experience. If you're a fellow sufferer, or if you've been one previously, hopefully you'll be able to see yourself in the picture I've been painting. But what is it actually *like* to live with these sensations? How does experiencing a constant dreaminess impact on someone's daily life? How does being emotionally numb affect...well, everything?

It's important to stress at this point (and this will be a central theme moving forwards) that everybody's experience of DPD is different – there's a lot of common ground but plenty of greyer areas too. This is also true for the condition's initial onset. Some find it appears suddenly and out of the blue, with debilitating and terrifying intensity, whereas for others (myself included) it's a far slower, more gradual decline over time. In my case, I use the analogy of it being like a staircase: my symptoms are constant for many months, then they suddenly worsen and that becomes my 'new normal'. Similarly, a lot of people describe physical analgesia and distortions to their vision ('seeing things in 2D', eye floaters, visual snow, loss of peripheral vision, etc.), whereas I don't really experience any of those things.

The initial haziness in 2008 was akin to the feeling of going away on holiday: you miss a night's sleep, catch the red-eye flight, land in an unfamiliar environment, force yourself to stay up to minimize jetlag, then have a couple of beers. You're sat over dinner feeling disorientated and struggling to comprehend a sense of time, but you know it's just exhaustion and you'll be fine the following morning.

I thought I'd burnt myself out at school and needed to catch up on sleep, but within a few months it was clear I had a problem that wasn't going away. In a sense the initial experience was bittersweet. Yes, it was confusing: I didn't know what was happening to me, I felt scared and I was convinced I had brain cancer. But it was also something that slightly worked to my advantage. In the same way having a couple of drinks might 'loosen you up' in social situations, the depersonalization had a similar effect on me. Part of it might just have been growing up and escaping school, but the onset was a much-needed loss of inhibitions for a terrified introvert whose main experience of other humans was being baited for their amusement. I remember saying to my first girlfriend that I felt the spaciness had 'improved me as a person'.

But of course, that's a tenuous silver lining in a cloud otherwise full of shit.

The loss of the sense of self is a constantly perturbing experience. Looking at my face in the mirror feels like an uncomfortable staring contest with a total stranger – most sufferers identify as feeling estranged from their own reflection and seeming separate from their body. Looking down now at my hands feels like the visuals of a first-person shooter game – it's just that I'm tapping on a keyboard rather than gripping a rifle. Sentences are appearing on the screen in front of me that logically I know I *must* be constructing in my head. But it feels like something else is controlling my hands; like I'm a puppet, and the words aren't anything I'm playing an active role in dreaming up. It's weird how diametrically opposed my feelings and logic can be.

This sense of unfamiliarity extends to people and places too (this is the derealization element of the condition). It's a horrible feeling to be looking at your partner – the person you know best in the world – and not *recognize* them. All the logic tells me I'm sat conversing with somebody I've known for years and I'm in a committed long-term relationship with. But very often, she feels like a complete stranger to me. I don't recognize her face. Her voice doesn't feel familiar. I'll be walking down the street holding her hand thinking, 'What on earth is going on? Who is this?' We'll discuss relationships in more detail soon, but this is indicative of the sorts of problems DPD can throw up.

To the outside world, sufferers often appear very 'normal'. As prominent DPD researcher Dr Mauricio Sierra describes it, 'the distressing complaints of patients with depersonalization do not seem accompanied by observable changes in behavior' (2009, p.132). I always think this is something of a blessing and a curse. On the one hand, it means I don't have to talk about it if I don't want to, and can usually make my way through short-term situations without people sussing that anything is wrong. The fact that I live with a chronic psychological disorder only has to be a topic of conversation if I choose it to be. However, the invisibility is also a nightmare for convincing people of how badly I'm struggling when I actually want to open up to them – medical professionals especially. I suppose this is a commonality of many mental illnesses. If you break a bone, people can see the evidence, so believing you is reinforced by their own judgement. When the 'break' is on the inside, they have a tendency to be a lot more sceptical.

Feeling as distant as I do and as emotionally flatlined as I am, it can be very hard to feel motivated about anything, even the things I know should be exciting or important. I'm certainly not a lazy person – I never have been – but nowadays even getting out of bed can be a struggle. I've always found it impossible to explain this lack of drive, because it's not representative of who I am. It's a complete consequence of feeling detached from reality. Essentially, nothing feels real enough to register in my mind as being worth caring about. I have a tendency to be frustratingly unproductive, even with things I would say I enjoy doing. Again, the idea of *knowing* what you're feeling without actually feeling it is such a confusing psychology. You just trust your instincts and go with the flow.

I also have to constantly fake enthusiasm for things, which can make me feel awful, but it's become a necessary part of bluffing my way through life. A friend telling you they've gotten engaged, your partner saying they love you, being given a thoughtful present on your birthday... Those should all be things that make your face light up. But when you don't feel any emotional response to hearing those words or unwrapping the gift (usually socks), the face wants to stay where it is and I can come across as heartless and ungrateful. I'm not – I really wish I could feel happy for my friends, I desperately want to be able to tell my partner I love her with genuine conviction, and everybody likes warm feet. I've had to learn to *pretend* my way through these situations. It might be perceived as insincere to do so – I suppose in some ways it's a coping strategy – but I hate the idea of my struggles impacting on others, so I consider it a white lie if anything. I don't like upsetting anybody if it isn't necessary.

A journalist once asked me during an interview, 'Are you acting?'

In the moment, I said no, but on reflection, life with DPD does feel like I'm playing a character, albeit one firmly rooted in the person I know I am. Los Angeles-based screenwriter and actress Jenny describes the differences between 'acting' through her depersonalization and playing a fictional character:

> I've always been very comfortable on stage and pretending to be other people. But I think it's scarier 'playing' yourself ... There's a self-judgement of 'This should be easier. Why is it so hard to embody myself?'... When you're playing a character, at least you feel somewhat present in that moment. When I'm having an episode of depersonalization, it feels more like I'm watching myself doing things, but I'm not present for it. I'm witnessing myself... I 'know' I'm in control, but I'm not 'feeling' in control.

Concentration is another area where I struggle badly. Maintaining trains of thought, finding the right words, applying myself to tasks and organizing my days to get jobs done are all things that have become increasingly hard. I frequently 'zone out' – sometimes for a half hour or more – and lose track of the day. Basic tasks take much longer to complete because I'm always getting sidetracked. Reading a book takes a huge amount of willpower as I need to go over each page several times to take in a small percentage of what it's saying to me. When I'm recording music or shooting a YouTube video, I make so many mistakes through my mind going blank that I have to keep scrapping takes. What should be a simple job ends up taking most of the day. I can be very forgetful – ask me to do something and the chances are I won't remember unless I set several alarms on my phone to remind me. These sorts of cognitive struggles are often referred to as 'brain fog', which I think is an apt description.

Interestingly, research has shown that in stressful situations people with depersonalization 'attach greater relevance to stimuli in irrelevant locations as they may be perceived as potentially threatening' (Schabinger *et al.* 2018, p.69). We become less able to differentiate extraneous 'noise' from important things, so everything is assumed to be a potential hazard that our consciousness needs to appraise.

I've always been a fairly tired person, but this has gotten worse to the point where I now have to take naps – unheard of for me until the last few years. Even simple things take so much mental energy and concentration that I quickly become exhausted, get bad headaches and must take to bed for a few hours. It sounds daft but I really have to budget my time and energy. If I have a long day coming up, I need an easy day and early night beforehand to prepare, and I make sure my diary is empty for a couple of days afterwards to recover. If I don't, I get killer headaches that even the strongest painkillers can't touch, and I literally can't function for throwing up. Long gone are the days where I could just slam a coffee and power through. This is one of the many obstacles to me being able to work regular hours or commit to things – it's a limitation that loves to watch me fail whenever I pretend I can ignore it. It can be so frustrating because I always want to do more.

I've never had the most active social life in the world, but as the depersonalization has gotten worse, I've found myself wanting to withdraw further. I've always found social situations wearying and need to balance them with alone time to recharge – that's just me being an introvert. But as I've gotten older, it's become more difficult to *want* to meet up with my friends, as the conversations have naturally become more 'grown up'. Instead of raving about a new album or partying, we now discuss their careers, mortgages and weddings, which can make me feel even worse about my situation.

It's not their fault, of course, and I understand no harm is ever meant by it. But hearing how well others are doing does have the effect of dragging you down when you're not exactly *adulting*. When I meet somebody for the first time, I'm now too old for them to lead with asking what I'm studying or whether I like football. It has inevitably become 'So, what do you do?' I say I'm a guitarist, but that only holds up for so long once they start digging. It quickly becomes obvious I'm not putting much food on the table with it.

There's a huge cloud of frustration overshadowing my life now because of how much I know I'm missing out on. Not being able to push myself as hard as I'd like to, not being able to earn enough money to support myself, not achieving things I once set out to achieve, not experiencing the dynamics of life's ups and downs, lacking ambition through nothing feeling real enough to be worth caring about, etc. I hate feeling like the awkward situation people tiptoe around, and being on the receiving end of pity, even though it's generally delivered with kind intentions. Everything I ever do feels confusing. I want to be able to make changes that I'm simply not able to make. It's like I've been suspended in time: I still feel like I'm 18 – definitely not a *grown-up*. I'm very aware that I'm losing so much of my life, and that is really fucking difficult to accept.

I'll be completely honest and say that in recent years, there have been times when it has all gotten too much and I've felt unable to cope. It's been common for me to go to bed not wanting to wake up in the morning, or wishing I could push a button and make myself disappear. During the writing of this book there have been times I've wanted to throw in the towel. I don't think I've been close to actioning these thoughts, but they've certainly been there.

In a nutshell, then: *Life with DPD is hell. Absolute hell.*

This has been a difficult chapter to write, but of course it's been a necessary one. I'm very keen for this book not to be too doom and gloom, but it would be misleading of me to gloss over the huge amount of suffering that comes with the condition and pretend it's not as debilitating and distressing as it is. It needed to be discussed – and I'm sorry if it was uncomfortable reading. But from now on in, let's try to focus on positively moving forwards by looking at what we can do to help ourselves. There's no better place to start with this than beginning to understand the science behind the condition.

4.
So What Is This Hell?

The Science behind DPD

Being able to describe the feelings and knowing how they can affect somebody are vital pieces of the puzzle, but they don't help us to *understand* what's actually going on. I'm no psychologist – my medical training consists of 30 minutes of first aid on a rubber mannequin – but reading the theory behind the condition and having a layman's grasp of what's likely going on inside my head has been an important step in the battle. It's reduced the fear of the unknown.

I always assumed the reason DPD is such an unknown phenomenon in comparison to other psychiatric disorders is because it's been a very recent discovery and awareness hasn't yet had a chance to get into textbooks and permeate through into medical training programmes, but that's far from true. Back in 1845, German neurologist Wilhelm Gresinger wrote: 'I see,... I hear, I feel, they say but the object doesn't reach me; I cannot receive the sensation; it seems to me as if there was a wall between me and the external world' (cited in Sierra 2009, p.8). Variations on the 'invisible barrier' metaphor have been used for nearly 200 years, even if it wasn't known specifically as depersonalization back then. It's certainly true to say, though, that professional interest in the condition remained low until the last few decades.

In the very simplest of terms, the mechanism of depersonalization is believed to be a protective 'reflex of the mind' (Baker *et al.* 2010, p.25) stemming from our evolutionary fight or flight response. In the same way that we'll instinctively raise our arms to shield ourselves if we expect a physical object to hit us, our mind can trigger depersonalization as a tool to improve our chances of survival. Human beings have a tendency to act erratically in stressful or traumatic circumstances as our systems become overwhelmed, so by numbing the gravity of the situation, we're better able to stay calm and use our available brainpower to escape rather than panic.

The most helpful analogy I've heard for this is that of an air-bag in a car (Bezzubova 2016). If you have an accident, the airbag deploys to cushion you from the physical impact and prevent you from getting hurt. Depersonalization is something of a 'psychological airbag'. When there's a sudden stress on the mind, the reflex can be triggered to protect us from the emotional impact. We're able to act, as per the metaphor, somewhat on autopilot; then, once the threat has gone, the autopilot disconnects. It's why you'll often find that if you're in the unfortunate car accident mentioned above, you'll be able to get out of the vehicle, speak with the person who hit you and swap details in a fairly calm and logical manner but then when you get home, you feel breathless and start trembling with shock. Depersonalization has done its job: it's helped you to calmly escape the situation, then process what's happened only once you're safe.

Dr Claudia Hallett, a Specialist Clinical Psychologist at the Maudsley Hospital Depersonalization Disorder Service, explains:

Depersonalization sensations can be a really normal response to stressful experiences in our life. One theory is that it is the brain's way of coping with stressful and overwhelming experiences by 'zoning out' and dampening down the emotional intensity of the experience.

If you've ever heard somebody describing getting a shock phone call saying that a friend has died, for example, you'll quite often hear phrases like 'It felt like a bad dream/It didn't feel as though it was really happening/I felt completely numb.' That person is likely describing depersonalization, and in the same language we sufferers do, because it's exactly the same. For them, at that time, it's a logical psychological response to the situation. The first 'stage' of grief is often said to be denial: perhaps that's because we're often so initially numbed that it doesn't seem real, rather than it being an unwillingness to accept a difficult truth.

Almost all of us will encounter this – and it's important to stress that depersonalization is definitely *not* always problematic – in an appropriate context, it can literally be the difference between life and death. In his excellent book *Into the Abyss*, Professor Anthony David, a cognitive neuropsychiatrist, Director of the UCL Institute of Mental Health and founder of the Maudsley DPD service, uses the analogy of this 'correct' depersonalization being 'like a valve opening which prevents the mind being overwhelmed by a surge of anxiety' (2020, p.46).

However, the response can become problematic if it starts to be triggered more than it's realistically needed. This is *transient depersonalization*: experiencing a temporary sense of detachment that comes and goes depending on the severity and duration of the primary factors causing it (of course, 'correct' depersonalization is technically transient in nature also). The reasoning is exactly the same as before in terms of it being a protective reflex. The mind becomes so overwhelmed with stressors that it feels the need to shield itself. Dr Elaine Hunter, Consultant Clinical Psychologist, senior research fellow at UCL and founder of thedepersonalisationclinic.com, offers a metaphor for the different elements of this reaction:

> I used to live in a house with a very sensitive electrical system - it would trip out all the time - and I think about depersonalization being a bit like that, switching off different circuits to protect the whole system. First, if you think of reality switching off, you can make everything dreamlike and feel not really 'here'. There's another switch of emotional reactivity: Let's switch off all emotions. Then, let's switch off how you feel physically. Somebody once gave me the beautiful description of feeling like they'd had a local anaesthetic but in their whole body. Nothing hurts anymore and you can't feel any sensations. Then, there's a cognitive input switch... To use a computer metaphor, you're running so many programs there's no spare capacity ... People can have a time where lots of stressors pile up, domino after domino, and they just start to feel periods of depersonalization. Or, there's a sudden surge where the system shuts down quickly, such as a panic attack.

If the base level of our cognitive 'current draw' (i.e., everything our mind is having to deal with during a certain period) is rising closer and closer to the point of troubling these psychological circuit breakers, even minor spikes of stress can then begin to trip the fuses. This is what is happening when people start to experience episodes of depersonalization. The mind has become so overwhelmed that it can't handle the demand without reflexively reducing it elsewhere.

You could think of it being like a reservoir with a dam: under normal circumstances water will just flow in, but if the dam is fit to burst, then a day of heavy rain could cause big problems if there isn't an outlet. Some people might only experience depersonalization like this the once. For others, it can happen more and more often whenever stressors begin to pile up.

Almost anything that raises our cognitive load, depending on what sort of person we are, can contribute to this process. Anxiety – and therefore panic – seems to be the most common factor, probably because it can come from all areas of our lives and in so many different forms. If we're feeling particularly on edge, or under threat from somebody or something, this can engulf our mind and prevent us from being able to focus on anything else as the survival instinct kicks in – almost like psychological tunnel vision. Stress is another factor, as is fatigue, overthinking, tendencies towards existential thoughts (questioning our place in the world, the meaning of life, what happens when we die, etc.) and drug use, to name but a few, although of course the spacey feeling we get from many recreational drugs can mirror the sensations of depersonalization.

More immediate factors will have an effect too: having an argument, trying to meet a deadline, giving a speech at work, starting a new job, being a performer waiting to go on stage, etc. These are usually the more transient 'spikes' that might ultimately trigger an episode of depersonalization. As Heather describes it:

> If I have a severe panic attack, I will 'leave my body' for an hour or two – but always return.

The mind doesn't necessarily need a triggering event to induce it, though – just for the level of overwhelm to max out.

So that's transient depersonalization: when the demand on the mind peaks, the fuses trip out. But once the cognitive load subsides (i.e., the overwhelm lessens and the fuses 'reset'), the sense of detachment goes away. It's *episodic* and the root cause is generally quite easy to identify – especially through the likes of Cognitive Behavioural Therapy (CBT) – as the depersonalization appears as a consequence of it. As we'll see later, identifying these primary causes and finding ways to reduce or manage them is key to reducing the frequency and severity of the depersonalization episodes.

But what about the chronic 24/7 depersonalization that I have: DPD? What's going on with the likes of me? I've had it solidly for over 12 years with not a single moment of clarity. Nothing 'triggers' it, nothing relieves it. It's always just *there*.

The mechanism is believed to be the same: it's still our mind trying to protect us. But the causes are generally much more complex and deep-rooted in our personality. In a way, the 'airbag' never deflates because it's trying to protect us from ourselves. Depersonalization becomes the primary diagnosis rather than it being a secondary symptom of other transient stressors. As an oversimplification, if the brain experiences prolonged stress and emotional upset for too long, eventually it decides it's had enough. This might be through a triggering event or a layering-up over time, but eventually the overwhelm and suffering become so bad that the mind decides life would be better without having to deal with it. So, out of self-preservation it flips the switch, but more permanently. If the world is a distressing place for an individual to be in, it would be much more tolerable – and survivable – if that pain were to just 'go away'. It makes sense: our mind has made our experience of life far more comfortable for us, like wrapping itself in emotional cotton wool. As far as our mind is concerned, it's done us a good turn.

However, by doing this – disengaging the sense of reality – the mind fundamentally changes our relationship with both ourselves and the outside world. In taking away our pain, it also takes away the meaning and experience. We become hollow, in a manner of speaking – detached entities that float around and don't relate to things like most other people do. I've previously described it as feeling like 'a constant anaesthetic of the mind'. Furthering the analogy in his book, Professor David writes that 'depersonalization and derealization might appear as a safety mechanism, but in an unlucky minority the valve "blows"– maybe the surge of anxiety was too strong ... and the state becomes fixed' (2020, p.47).

The underlying factors driving chronic DPD can be very different from one individual to the next but are often traced back – at least in part – to emotional difficulties experienced during childhood: a stressful family life, bullying at school, peer ostracization, relocating so often that it was hard to form friendships, more severe child abuse, etc., and the corresponding thought patterns and self-beliefs those issues instil in us. In the next chapter we'll be looking closer at how our sense of self is formed, but if a child's emotional needs aren't met, then that can bring about an inherent anxiety in their personality. As a consequence, adaptive behaviours and thought patterns begin to form, the problems perpetuate and the child will likely develop negative self-beliefs. My school experience taught me that other humans are nasty, so I avoided them and learned to hate myself as a result of feeling like my personality was broken. Needless to say, troubled children often grow up to be troubled adults, and once those sorts of traits are drilled into somebody, they can be very difficult to challenge, even with professional help. I was suffering and wanted to disappear – and, in a sense, that happened.

Dr Hunter explains:

> People often use two adjectives about when their depersonalization starts: 'overwhelmed' and 'trapped' – and this combination seems to trigger the depersonalization response. This is also what happens when people experience trauma as well – people I was interviewing [during her PhD in childhood trauma] had repetitive trauma, so they couldn't get away. It was often within the family and they knew it was coming. So, they needed to psychologically escape because they couldn't escape physically.

Sometimes this more 'fixed' state of unreality is people's first-time experience of the sensations. That's how it happened for me: once the haze was in my mind, it was there for good – 'my valve blew'. But it can also be the case that people who experience transient depersonalization – that child needing to psychologically escape, for example – find their episodes begin to perpetuate into a chronic disorder. Dr Emma Černis, a clinical psychologist and Wellcome Trust clinical doctoral fellow at the Oxford University Department of Psychiatry, explains how the mind's repeated use of its protective mechanism can lead to dissociation becoming a sort-of 'default' escape.[1] It transitions from being part of the initial fight or flight response to the more dissociative 'freeze' response of damage limitation:

> You have this anxiety response – the 'fight or flight' thing – where your body is full of adrenaline and energizes everything, but once your brain realizes you can't escape, it essentially switches to harm minimization [and dissociates] ... The thinking is, if you've had that experience, your body is more practised at getting into

---

1   Dr Černis is referencing Schauer and Elbert (2010).

that, and it learns how to get into it quicker and quicker each
time - until the point that small triggers and mild anxiety can turn
on that whole response. So, what might start out as being a direct
trauma response can become a learnt, over-rehearsed response.

The trauma element to DPD is a statistically significant one, which
has been a stumbling block for me in terms of understanding my
own particular case. I think generally in society we associate the word
'trauma' with sudden and extreme events, such as getting attacked,
being in an accident, being sexually assaulted, being in war zones, etc.
Of course, that's all true - and chronic depersonalization can absolutely be a response to post-traumatic stress disorder (PTSD). Ute
Lawrence, Chair of the PTSD Association of Canada, experienced
depersonalization for years as a response to being involved in a huge
car accident in which she witnessed people burn to death (Lawrence
2015). She had already experienced episodes of dissociation as a child
to cope with an abusive parent, and trauma specialist Dr Bessel Van
Der Kolk wrote about her in his acclaimed book *The Body Keeps the
Score*, detailing:

> [At] some point Ute discovered that she could blank out her mind
> when her mother yelled at her. Thirty-five years later, when she was
> trapped in her demolished car, Ute's brain automatically went into the
> same survival mode - she made herself disappear. (2014, p.72)

So, extreme trauma can absolutely trigger the mechanism. But it's
taken me a long time to understand that trauma can very much
apply to less immediate, more prolonged scenarios as well. Trauma
isn't necessarily over in a few intense minutes. Knowing about the
link with trauma and having looked into it with several therapists,

I used to be confused because I was unable to think of any stand-out event from my life that I'd classify as being overly 'traumatic' in the drastic sense of the word. But that doesn't necessarily mean my DPD is separate from trauma. Prolonged bullying, repeated rejection, the loss of a loved one, businesses going bankrupt, bad relationships, belligerent parents, financial worries, arguments with friends, friction with colleagues... All of those things can cause psychological trauma too. Plus, it's quite often these more sustained, 'lower-level' experiences that seem to be most prevalent in DPD patients (psychologists would colloquially differentiate them as being 'Big T' and 'Little T' traumas).

It's important to say that, as with so many of these things, DPD can exist separately from trauma – an absence of trauma in a personal history doesn't predetermine a negative diagnosis. Dr Černis adds:

> If you don't believe you've had a trauma but you do have depersonalization, I wouldn't advocate that you go looking for trauma. My fear is that people start thinking they 'should' have a trauma. It's very unpopular to say that you can have dissociation without trauma ... It can absolutely be the cause, but not necessarily for everybody.

Depression is another significant factor in DPD, which again, makes sense from a theoretical standpoint: our mind doesn't want us to feel low in mood, especially long term, because it's painful, and it can stop the pain by numbing our reality and emotions. Depressed people can find they first experience transient depersonalization during times where things are especially bad, but if the depression is deep, long and painful enough, it can become chronic. Professor David adds:

Low mood is common in people with depersonalization and a key symptom of depression is anhedonia - the inability to feel pleasure. People with depersonalization get this too, although it also seems to encompass the inability to feel unpleasant emotions as well.

In 2019, British journalist and former political aide Alastair Campbell made a documentary about depression, having suffered with it for most of his life. In it, he describes the experience as 'when you're at your lowest, there's an overwhelming feeling of being on your own, even if you're surrounded by other people. It's as if you've been unplugged from the world.' The fundamental sense of disconnection and nothingness might be another commonality between the two conditions. It's easy to imagine how being repeatedly subjected to a sudden crash in mood, or a continual void of emptiness, could be something our mind would want to protect us from.

All of these things are different paths into exactly the same mechanism. They all overwhelm the mind and cause a person to experience a prolonged emotional distress they feel unable to escape from. Eventually, the mind feels it has to do something to ease the suffering, and so 'switches off' reality out of self-preservation. Spending my years at school constantly on red alert kept my brain in a prolonged state of heightened anxiety. My fight or flight response was activated repeatedly - embarrassingly, the frequent diarrhoea proves that (Morgan 2016) - perhaps to the point where it shifted to the 'freeze' response of damage limitation. Some of the incidents *might* have caused 'Little T' traumas. Before the DPD set in, I always felt incredibly low in mood. I felt rejected. I believed I was defective. I was never happy. There was no escaping any of it. So, in terms of stressors, constant overwhelm and risk factors, I pretty much ticked all of the boxes. DPD being triggered seems a fairly logical outcome, given everything going on for me during those years.

We'll explore this deeper in Chapter 6, but the use of recreational drugs – cannabis in particular – is a very common trend surrounding the initial onset of DPD. I've heard from many people who have said to me they've taken drugs and 'never really come down from the high'. I guess the same could potentially be said for me. The link is significant but, in short, it's believed the drugs themselves don't 'cause' DPD. However, the experience of being under the influence and how we might psychologically react to a bad trip into the panicky unknown can definitely contribute. As Dr Elena Bezzubova, a California-based psychoanalyst with depersonalization expertise, puts it: '[D]epersonalization frequently emerges after marijuana intake. However, "after" does not mean "because"' (2019).

The brain science behind depersonalization is, as you might guess, *slightly* complicated, and also limited in its research. For people who might be thinking they're experiencing something that nobody else does, knowing that the effects can be seen in brain scans (albeit in a tentative way) can be validating. Professor David, who is largely responsible for kickstarting studies in this complex area, elaborates:

> We only have some preliminary research to go by and a lot of interpretation. A fairly robust finding is the lack of physiological arousal that people with depersonalization show (such as reduced skin conductance – like a lie detector test). The brain is continually logging and interpreting the information that comes from inside the body, as well as what comes from outside, through the senses. This 'internal sense' is called interoception. It is generally accepted that the insula (a part of the cerebral cortex at the join

between the frontal lobe and the temporal lobe) plays a key role in this. It is complicated because there is a two-way link between the rest of the body and the brain.

Not only does the brain pick up and monitor what's going on 'down below', but it also links thoughts and emotions (in the brain or mind) to the body so that it may react appropriately. The amygdala is the brain's fear centre, so our strongest emotions seem to come from that. We think that part of the frontal lobes is there to control emotions – to appraise them ('Is this something really bad or is it OK?') and to try and 'steady' our responses. Not enough control and we will swing from emotion to emotion and feel at their mercy. Too much control and we don't respond enough, perhaps feeling 'numb' or that the world is lacking in life (a bit like depersonalization). So, we think that something has gone wrong in this circuit – either there is a general lack of responsivity, or there is too much – but how this complicated circuit of checks and balances goes awry we don't know.

So, although the details of how it all works are still quite sketchy, those observations would seem to logically back up the 'as if' sensations we experience. If both the amygdala (the brain's *alarm*) and insula (largely responsible for our perceptions and interoception – arguably, our *sense of self*) are underactive, that would explain the lack of emotions, the numbing of reality and feeling separated from our lived experiences. But at the same time, the pre-frontal cortex – which regulates the whole system – could be overactive, ensuring those already suppressed areas remain firmly pinned down, as well as worsening our tendencies towards overthinking. This gives us a triple-whammy effect of numbing, excessive control and obsessive thought patterns. Dr Černis explains further:

> In dissociation, you see the amygdala acting as an alarm system, but then the pre-frontal cortex activates even more ... and pours a load of cold water on it. So that's where it's thought the dissociative numbness comes from: the front of your brain going, 'No! You're not doing that!' and 'cancelling' the experience.

Additionally, Dr Van Der Kolk notes that, especially in instances of trauma, the thalamus – the area of the brain 'helping you distinguish between sensory information that is relevant and information that you can safely ignore' (2014, p.70) – can shut down too if sensory signals are interrupted or not able to be 'sorted'. Every stimulus (including irrelevant background noises) will need to be given conscious consideration to assess them, which can be exhausting and lead us to struggle with concentration. I used to love listening to music as I worked but now have to have silence – my attention constantly attaches to the sound and I can't apply myself elsewhere.

Interestingly, Dr Černis explained to me that the amygdala – the alarm system – is very old in terms of our evolution, which means it's almost entirely sensory; it doesn't really 'work' with words. This means that being our 'fear centre', its job is to alert us to danger. But to do that, it relies on stirring up sensory memories rather than verbal ones. This goes a good way towards explaining why the likes of panic attacks, and therefore *some* episodes of depersonalization, can be triggered by things we smell, or just the way somebody moves. They set off the alarm through sensory association.

Although I know people who have experienced DPD since they were young children and others who experienced it only in later life, DPD most commonly comes on during the teenage years – 16 being the average age of onset (Simeon *et al.* 1997). This is the time in our lives where stress levels and anxiety typically ramp up as we transition from bubble-wrapped children into independent adults and suddenly find ourselves with lots of extra responsibilities: higher education, employment, mortgages, adult relationships, children, etc. However, as Dr Hunter points out:

> That's also often when people are experimenting with drugs for the first time.

Without the drug-trigger component, we might see less of a cluster in that age group.

One person who definitely did experience a sudden and overwhelming change in circumstances at this point in their life was dodie, who began to suffer with DPD around the exact time her career started to take off.

> I think sometimes it might have triggered it. It added up to this crazy year of 'My dreams came true? What?' It was just so big. I was receiving letters, performing shows, people would look at me as if I was famous...and it was just so 'not right' in my world as I'd grown up thinking it'd never happen. So, when it did, I couldn't wrap my head around it.

I've often wondered whether certain types of people might be more predisposed to developing DPD than others. An early study led by American psychiatrist and leading DPD researcher Dr Daphne Simeon (Simeon et al. 1997) suggested there was a higher prevalence in females, although it was speculated that may have been due to females being more likely to seek evaluation or treatment for a mental health condition. However, a later study (Simeon et al. 2003) found more conclusively that, in terms of gender, the split was generally equal between male and female. More recent research has shown a high prevalence of depersonalization in people with gender dysphoria – but more on that in Chapter 5.

I've probably spoken to over a hundred DPD sufferers over the years, and I typically ask them about what sort of person they'd say they are. In doing so, I've felt I've seen some trends emerging. I'm definitely sceptical about how much value the Myers-Briggs Type Indicator (MBTI®)[2] system has, aside from giving employers a vague overview of their job applicants, but I've taken several of those tests and always come out very conclusively as the 'rarest' personality type of the '16 Personalities': INFJ (Introversion, iNtuition, Feeling and Judgement).[3] In the early days of *DPD Diaries* I asked people to take one of these tests, and everybody who did came out as INFJ too – or at most, a single letter different. Fewer than 1 per cent of people are INFJs and yet DPD sufferers seemed to be regularly getting that result.

I felt this reinforced what I'd been seeing. Almost everybody would tell me they're substantially introverted, are (or, pre-DPD, were) sensitive and emotional people, are very driven to achieve their goals and would modestly admit they're above average intelligence. To me, the 'classic' DPD sufferer would be a quiet, bright, compassionate, highly analytical idealist who is fairly socially withdrawn and, in the majority of cases, creative. A recent study of performing artists found that participants with DPD 'had significant elevated

---

2   A diagnostic questionnaire that aims to analyse a person's character and fundamental personality – resulting in an abbreviation which differentiates between four pairings of traits: Introversion vs. Extraversion; Sensing vs. iNtuition; Thinking vs. Feeling; and Judging vs. Perceiving. Examples would be ENTP, ISFJ, etc.
3   '16 Personalities' (nd) 'Who is an advocate (INFJ)?' Accessed 7 April 2020 at www.16personalities.com/infj-personality.

shame and creative anxiety' (Thompson and Jaque 2020, p.7) – strong negative schemas that might also explain what drives many of us to express ourselves artistically.

Before getting too carried away with my theory, I mention it to Dr Hunter, who offers a few words of caution:

> Literally anybody can get depersonalization ... That would maybe fit with what I'm saying about anxious people, but then there's some who don't really show that at all – especially the drug-trigger people: happy-go-lucky, then have a horrible experience and life changes from then on. I don't think there's a one-size-fits-all approach.

It's not quite so clear cut after all then, as she has professionally spent over 20 years assessing many hundreds of people with DPD from all different backgrounds and walks of life. But perhaps it could still be a vague indicator, especially without the drug-trigger element.

Our personal thinking styles can absolutely play into DPD. A common theme among sufferers – while not one I personally experience – is that of *existentialism*: obsessive deep thoughts about the nature of life, the universe, space, death, etc. Jen, a sufferer, explained:

> I honestly can't imagine DPD without existential thoughts: thinking about the nature of consciousness, what it 'feels like' to exist, the fact that one day I won't exist. At the same time, concepts of eternity and space (literal outer space) are also part of this existential dread ... I think it's more that the DPD generates the existential thoughts, for me ... It feels like a complete separation from mind, body and soul. It's brought about a sense of panic that I'm stuck in a weird state between life and death.

Some sufferers mentioned that films encouraging this way of thinking, such as *The Matrix* and *Shutter Island*, have been major triggers for them. These thought patterns can overwhelm our minds and lead us to worry excessively about concepts out of our control.

Anxiety, too, can be broken down into subsections – and the likes of OCD are common amongst DPD sufferers as thought processes that exacerbate things. We'll see in Chapter 10 that compulsively monitoring symptoms can be problematic in terms of recovering from the condition, so a predisposition towards that can be an issue. Dr Hunter adds:

> Anxiety is an umbrella term for lots of different types of anxiety. Social anxiety, generalized anxiety disorder, OCD, panic and agoraphobia, health anxiety... They're all types. So, OCD is part of the anxiety pattern – and sometimes the obsessive thinking can become about the symptoms of depersonalization.

As with the existentialism, this can form a cognitive feedback loop, of sorts.

Depersonalization has been known to come on during a period of illness or following the birth of a child. There are several schools of thought on why both of these can be precursors, but it's likely because they're both typically periods of incredibly high stress, anxiety and fatigue. Fiona Godlee, Editor-in-Chief of the *British Medical Journal*, experienced DPD as a response to childbirth. She explained in a *BMJ* podcast how 'bathing my baby... They didn't look like my hands. I had that sense from then on ... a feeling of looking through a clear fog' (Adlington *et al.* 2017). Becoming a parent is incredibly overwhelming and exhausting, and involves a lot of physical and hormonal changes for the mother. Potential links with postnatal depression shouldn't be ignored either – 10 per cent of women experience some form of perinatal mental health issues (Morgan 2016). There can also be a trauma element, as Dr Hallett details:

> Childbirth can be a particularly mentally vulnerable time for women, and depending on how they experienced their birth, they may be left with feelings of trauma or detachment from the birth experience and have difficulties connecting to their child.

Being ill is also something that can cause intense worry: what's ailing you, your workload piling up whilst you're stuck in bed, who's going to look after the kids, etc. Perhaps having the 'flu whilst pushing for my Music finals wasn't completely blameless in the onset of my DPD. A friend of dodie underwent heart surgery. He then had a panic attack, thought it was his heart going wrong, and that triggered his depersonalization. Another sufferer I spoke with had the onset of their DPD coincide with an oesophageal operation. Anything of a medical nature can be frightening – something our mind might feel it needs to protect us from.

A big area of worry for DPD sufferers – especially early on – is thinking the symptoms might be being caused by a physical problem in the brain. It's important to highlight that in the majority of cases DPD has psychological causes. However, Professor David has encountered patients with depersonalization (or at least, depersonalization-*like* symptoms) stemming from physical roots:

> Migraine is one, and temporal lobe epilepsy is another. Very rarely a stroke (or brain injury) can cause damage to a very specific part of the brain connecting sensory input with emotional evaluation – causing disconnection. Whether this is depersonalization, or

something that resembles depersonalization but is not the same, is a matter of debate. The suddenness of onset of depersonalization in some people makes them think it must be something like a stroke – but in my experience no evidence for one is ever found.

It's for this reason I'd always recommend having brain scans if they're an option during the course of your treatment. The chances are they'll come back negative but they can give both patient and clinician peace of mind before completely committing to psychological therapy. Alina explains:

When the neurologist heard about my symptoms, he insisted a head injury or a tumour must be the cause ... but when he'd ruled out any physical issues with my brain, he concluded my symptoms must be psychological.

Again, physical causes are statistically low, but if you suffer from migraines or epilepsy, it's relevant to be aware of the potential link and discuss that with a neurologist.

As well as knowing what depersonalization is, it's important to consider what it *is not*. People experiencing symptoms often worry they might be becoming schizophrenic – or simply 'going crazy'. Hopefully by now we've established that depersonalization is a normal psychological reaction, albeit an unwanted and persistent one, so we're definitely not going 'crazy'. It's not a 'malfunction' as such – more a bodyguard that's become a little heavy-handed. However, it should go without saying that when it comes to getting a diagnosis for *any* psychiatric condition, there's no substitute whatsoever for seeking a professional opinion.

Schizophrenia has been described as when a person 'may not be able to distinguish their own thoughts and ideas from reality' (NHS, 2020), and this notion of it being an alteration in reality perception can lead DPD sufferers to panic. However, there are two important defining characteristics typically exhibited by individuals suffering with psychotic disorders: hallucinations and delusions. Whist it *is* possible for depersonalization to be part of the experience of schizophrenia, the presence of these characteristics are what typically set the psychosis and dissociation spectrums apart. Professor David explains further:

> [DPD] is not a disorder of belief – the sufferer does not believe things about the world that most others disagree with ... People with schizophrenia – often in the early stages – feel that their mind (and body) is changing in some subtle way. They may start to see the world differently from others. But the person believes that the world (or themselves) is actually changing. Schizophrenia almost always includes other symptoms, including hallucinations – particularly auditory (that is, 'hearing voices'). Often the voices talk to, or about, the person in a derogatory way. People with schizophrenia also suffer from cognitive impairments – of quite a severe kind – not just a slight dulling of intellect. Their thinking can become confused and hard for others to follow. None of these symptoms are part of depersonalization.

One professor who has been looking into this more closely is Dr Elizabeth Pienkos of Clarkson University in New York – I was recently part of her investigations into the similarities and differences between DPD and schizophrenia spectrum disorders. The final papers from this research haven't yet been published at the time of writing, but I've seen the preliminary summary – which included a phrase I think sums up the fundamental difference between the two so beautifully. She notes that DPD sufferers in the study generally exhibited 'a strong commitment to the reality of the world in spite of these profound changes'. I'm not sure there has ever been a better description of the plight of the depersonalized individual than maintaining a commitment to reality despite feeling completely removed from it.

This is the key differentiator between DPD and schizophrenia. Sufferers of depersonalization are still very much rooted in the *real world* in terms of our thoughts and actions, which is why the condition can be so invisible. Our *reality-testing* is intact. This isn't typically the case for psychotic disorders – behaviours may visibly change, and thoughts become distorted or confused. Further, people with psychosis will typically believe their delusions or 'overvalued ideas' very strongly, whereas with DPD we're very aware that the ways in which we're perceiving things are 'incorrect'. Both the American Psychiatric Assocation's *Diagnostic and Statistical Manual of Mental Disorders (DSM-5)* and the World Health Organization's *International Classification of Diseases (ICD-10-CMP)* guidelines state that in DPD/DDS, the patient needs to recognize that the condition only affects their feelings about the world – not the way the world really is (Baker *et al.* 2010).

It's interesting to consider that, despite the marked differences between the two, certain traits of the psychosis and dissociative spectrums can have an overlap, and sufferers struggling to verbalize their sensations highlight this ambiguity. Dr Černis, who has recently published a paper on dissociative experiences in psychosis (2020), explains:

In some places, it's hard to distinguish what could be a psychotic thought and what could be a dissociative thought. One person from the qualitative interview study really stands out to me, because when he was very unwell, he would say he was 'the second coming of Christ' – and I have no doubt that had I met him then, he would have met criteria for a [psychotic] delusion. But years later in the interview with me, he explained that was the only way he could describe how he felt. So there's this very blurry boundary between whether he really believed that and it was a delusion, or did he just come across as delusional because he was trying to describe a dissociative sensation of feeling transcended and the only thing he could think of to say was that he felt like a messiah? He was talking a lot about how the things he said might not be interpreted as intended by the person hearing it. Teasing that distinction apart is hard.

The complexity in describing sensations is one of the big reasons why DPD is still largely unknown in medical circles. Patients find them difficult to verbalize, meaning misdiagnosis is incredibly common, and clinicians might not always be able to interpret what we say in the manner we intend. We also need to be careful, as the frantic quest to identify our symptoms – especially if we haven't yet received a formal diagnosis – might lead us to be hyper-analytical and take us down the path of wanting to find evidence of conditions regardless. I definitely used to Google conditions and actively try to apply the symptoms to myself out of desperation to give my struggles a name. My problem of confusing dreams with reality, for example, is a fairly logical byproduct of real life feeling dreamlike through dissociation. But in the past it was something I would want to put down to delusional thoughts, because even a diagnosis of schizophrenia would have given me direction in regard to seeking help. It's natural to want to understand what's happening to you but it's dangerous to jump to conclusions based on confirmation bias.

There can potentially be other areas of our health that can contribute to DPD – or at least, depersonalization-*like* symptoms – although many of these are still little understood. Dr Simeon wrote in 2004 that 'mood, anxiety and personality disorders are often comorbid with depersonalization disorder, but none predict symptom severity' (p.343) and also noted that imbalances in neuro-chemicals and hormones can potentially play a part. One sufferer I know was diagnosed with Lyme disease – a key symptom of which can be 'cognitive decline' (Healthline 2017). I've often thought that being a lifelong vegetarian could be a factor for me – lacking a certain vitamin or protein, for example. Bacteria in the gut can impact your mood – I once went on the anti-candida diet in case toxicity from a yeast overgrowth was affecting my brain function. So, there can be alternative paths into the long-term sensations that aren't necessarily primary DPD. Again, it's important to discuss these possibilities with a trained medical professional.

A comment I've seen come up many times on forums and videos I've made is 'DPD is 100 per cent an anxiety disorder'. However, the simple premise of it being a primary diagnosis rather throws doubt on this. Dr Hunter explains:

> It's often triggered by anxiety, but it *is* separate ... I've rarely met anyone with depersonalization who doesn't have 'some' issues with anxiety. But for people who are depressed and 'don't want to be me anymore', anxiety isn't so much a part of that picture. So, they [depersonalization and anxiety] are 'conjoined twins' in a lot of people but are still their own separate entities.

Varying forms of anxiety – and therefore panic – are often significant contributors, especially to transient depersonalization. But it isn't correct to attribute depersonalization entirely to anxiety in every instance.

A final part of the wider problem is that the whole DPD process can very much be self-perpetuating. If you have a panic attack, the experience of imploding from an overwhelm of anxiety can be terrifying. But you can then begin to worry about having another panic attack, which raises your anxiety levels, which makes you more susceptible to triggers, which makes it more likely that you'll have another panic attack, and that can result in it becoming a panic disorder. The same is very true for depersonalization – we might experience it transiently, but those experiences might be distressing. If we then begin to worry and obsess about experiencing it again, that fear can begin to trip the switch...and as we know, the more the response is triggered, the easier it can become for our mind to default to it as a regular coping mechanism.

Identifying these thought patterns is the fundamental premise to much of the psychological therapy that exists to combat DPD. The key to recovery is breaking the endless cycle, interrupting the thoughts and beliefs driving it forward, and giving ourselves a skillset to better control them. Very often, simply understanding the psychology we've discussed here and being less scared of the sensations as a result can heavily contribute to that process. As the saying goes, knowledge is power.

5.
Loss or Disruption?

The Sense of Self

One of the most common phrases used by academics when discussing DPD is 'the sense of self', and it's long been said that the condition is best described as a loss of it. As a sufferer, it's one of those phrases I can absolutely identify with, whilst simultaneously not really understanding what it means. What is a sense of self? How does a human being get one? And what might have gone wrong in DPD for us to have lost it?

I meet with philosopher Dr Anna Ciaunica on a stormy Sunday afternoon in London. Much of her research has been centred around this concept, and after a three-bean chilli pub-meal, we begin to explore the basics of this deep conceptual idea that's central to much of modern philosophy. I had a philosophy lesson at school once. I got asked, 'Does this table know it's a table?' Apparently my reply, 'Of course it doesn't – it's a bloody table!', meant I'd be studying physics instead. I hope I can keep up. Dr Ciaunica explains:

> Our experiences are tacitly accompanied by a sense of self, which is typically taken for granted because it's always there.

> Think of a window that's so clean and so transparent that it gives you the impression you're directly in contact with the outside world. Under normal conditions you don't see it's there and you experience a sense of immersiveness into the world. Now, imagine there is a crack in the window, like the ones you have on trains. The glass will crack into tiny little particles which render opaque your access to the world. The landscape is hindered; its clarity is lost. So, there is a disconnection and a loss of the tacit, transparent immersiveness. However, saying that one 'loses' one's sense of self can be misleading. The self is still there; it's just that it's disrupted ... You will always experience the world through your own first-personal perspective, and that's something you can't escape from ... Most of the time when you try to understand what's happening to you, you try to understand what is happening to *you*. You go on to search for the 'lost' self from your own self-perspective, not mine. What is 'lost' is the way one experienced one's self previously. That self-experience is transformed - the glass is cracked - but it doesn't disappear. It exists under a different form.

Straight away, this throws that basic premise of us having 'lost our sense of self' into question. It surely can't be accurate to say that, despite the overwhelming sense of unreality with which we live our lives, when we still have our own preferences, traits and desires. I've had DPD solidly for many years but I can still tell you that I enjoy Margherita pizzas, I like things to be neat and tidy, and I want Lewis Hamilton to win the Formula 1 again this year. By definition, these individualistic idiosyncrasies must be a reflection of a *self*. Depersonalization doesn't fundamentally alter who we are as a person. If it did, the condition wouldn't be as invisible from the outside as it is.

As personalities and physical entities, we stay largely the same, but the way we perceive our first-person experiences is altered. It therefore seems far more accurate to describe DPD as a *disruption in the sense of self*, rather than a whole loss.

As children, the accepted measure for having developed a sense of self is the mirror test – or rouge test – developed by psychologist Gordon Gallup Jr in 1970. A young child is placed in front of a mirror and allowed to observe themselves. They then have a dot of make-up placed upon their forehead. Until the age of approximately 18 months, the child will see the dot appear and reach out towards it in the mirror, but after this point, they've formed an understanding that the image they're seeing is a reflection of themselves and will reach up towards the dot on their own forehead instead. They have developed a conscious sense of self and recognize themselves as an object from a third-person perspective. However, Dr Ciaunica proposes an alternative perspective to this decades-old idea:

> Human beings experience basic forms of self-awareness that are in place way before the mirror self-recognition stage. These forms are not based on visuo-spatial modes of recognition. Rather, they involve the most basic sense with which we begin our life journey, in the womb: namely the touch. Prenatally and after birth, infants spend a lot of time exploring their bodies and their closer environment. As it happens, in humans, the closer environment is necessarily an other's body. Without the constant physical presence of a caregiver, human infants are bound to die very quickly. This means that the first encounters are made skin-to-skin, way before we meet others face to face. In early life infants form a sense of 'me' being distinct from others literally through others' bodies.

She holds her hand out and looks in the opposite direction.

> If you don't know exactly where your hand is, what do you do?

She places it down on the table.

> You contrast it against something else. The contrast between what is 'not me' gives key information of where the 'I' is located. I think this is precisely what's happening in childhood – the multisensory presence of others provides us with an ongoing contrast against which we get more information about the developing 'I'.

The idea of our sense of self largely being formed during childhood definitely plays into the trend of DPD sufferers typically holding negative self-beliefs. The analogy of a child's personality being like putty is a terrible cliché, but if we are in a safe, nurturing environment and receiving positive feedback from our parents and peers, our self-esteem and sense of who we are will develop in a healthy and 'normal' way without excessive anxiety or emotional upset to disrupt the process.

However, as Dr Van Der Kolk explains, 'If you feel safe and loved, your brain becomes specialized in exploration, play and cooperation; if you are frightened and unwanted, it specializes in managing feelings of fear and abandonment' (2014, p.56). If we encounter significant rejection and hostility during our formative years, our beliefs about ourselves are still shaped by the external feedback of others. Every berating will rip the scab off the emotional injury and lead us further down the path of believing the insults are truth. As we naturally begin to associate other humans with pain, behavioural patterns of avoidance and isolation set in as the self-preservation fuse is lit – and you end up hiding on a stone step. The opposite can be true, too: if a parent is over-protective and wary of giving a child independence, this can also hamper the formative processes as the child forms an unhealthy attachment and separation anxiety, and their independent *self* falls below the line simply by virtue of it not being necessary to develop it. Raising an emotionally healthy child is a tough balancing act – and one that relies on many areas of their life being simultaneously nurturing and safe. Dr Černis adds:

> In my work [mainly focusing on dissociation in the context of psychosis] I'm looking for a common cause, so people who do and don't have trauma can understand what caused it [dissociation] – and those things seem to be centred around emotional regulation, which obviously gets severely affected in trauma ... but can come from all sorts of other experiences too. Parenting teaches kids a lot about emotions, for example. So, if you were inadvertently never taught how to 'do' emotions, had emotions dismissed or felt unable to talk about them, or maybe had a highly emotional parent and found that upsetting, your relationship to emotions is going to be a bit different. Perhaps, as a result, emotions are confusing or even threatening and so you shut them down or get in a tangle trying to cope with them. This is all early stages, but people are beginning to point at emotional regulation being a factor, whether or not they think that trauma is the reason.

In an article for *Aeon* magazine in 2018, Dr Ciaunica made reference to the work of the philosopher Edmund Husserl, who presented the idea of differentiating between the subjective experience of a body as lived from a first-personal perspective (the *Leib*, or 'body-as-subject') and as perceived from an external perspective (the *Körper*, or 'body-as-object'). For example, an anorexic person may experience their body as being fat, while objectively it's thin. For most people, our internal perception naturally feels more 'real' to us as it's our *own* experience – so is it the case in instances of depersonalization that reality of the roles has been reversed, or even that the *Leib* has done a runner?

> Our sense of self is like a well-made cocktail: it has to have the right ingredients to be tasty. My suggestion is that in depersonal-ization there is an imbalance between the first- and third-person perspective, with an excessive weight put on the latter. What I think is really important is the ability to flexibly switch between the two ... If that mediating and flexible bridge is altered, what do you do? You try hard to figure out what's going on [and] what went wrong. In doing so, you inadvertently may fuel the thinking machinery that puts you into an 'object'-like perspective: you take yourself as an object of an enquiry. And you disrupt the tacit transparent connection that you have with your self as a subject of an experience. My favourite example is when you dance to your favourite tune, fully immersed into your bodily movements and the music. Now, imagine your boss enters the room. You can sud-denly 'see' your self through the other's eyes. Your immersiveness is disrupted and you may end up dancing in an artificial, 'fake' manner. This might be the case for depersonalization: to have an 'other' simultaneously and constantly checking on your 'self'. But that 'other' is still you, and you know it. It must be exhausting.

As mentioned before, simple tasks – and especially social situations – take so much mental energy that I feel tired constantly, so this is certainly something that makes sense for me. I definitely should have answered 'yes' when that reporter asked me if I was acting my way through life a few years back, because in many ways all DPD sufferers are. We instinctively know – or perhaps remember – *who* our self is, despite not being on first-name terms with them anymore. So instead, we play their character. We know how they should behave, speak and move. We understand their sense of humour and traits. People living with chronic DPD are *understudies*, of sorts, promoted to the limelight as the star of the show is now poorly and can't make the matinee. Again, you're operating on what you instinctively know, and are trusting your learned logic rather than going by what you feel. As Jenny describes it:

> It's almost like when you're high, and you're thinking, 'Don't act high! Stop acting high! You're acting high!' Except it's, 'Be normal! Walk normal! Breathe normal!' You're trying to regulate all these things, thinking, 'I don't know how I usually do this!'

A similar perspective is shared by dodie:

> I feel like I'm really good at acting sober when I'm drunk, because it's the same thing. You just have to function through.

It seems a bit like when aliens come to earth in sci-fi films and take over the body of a human: they have to learn the protocols of the species and try not to stand out too much by suddenly devouring a dog, or something. Even basic tasks require a huge amount of careful consideration to get them 'right'.

If we're perpetually acting our way through the DPD, does this give us more of an ability to change the external perceptions of our sense of self: the *Körper*? Can we shapeshift ourselves into different characters? This isn't a concept specific to DPD – many will identify with it, regardless of potential mental illness – but it's an interesting thought. Jane and I have had many chats about this over the years. She believes she adapts her personality in every social situation, depending on who she's with:

> I feel quite chameleon-like. I've always been comfortable trying on different hats and then coming back to 'me' in the centre … For me, depersonalization takes away that inner life and leaves you just with that externality, bouncing things off other people to validate that you exist. I think the sense of really 'living' is the internal experience – and that's gone.

On the flipside, I would say that in terms of behaviour and mannerisms, I'm *exactly* the same person in every situation, regardless of whether I'm down the pub with my mates or chatting with my 90-year-old grandma. I might swear a little less in the latter instance, but my vocabulary and tendencies towards finding the inappropriately funny side of situations are unchanged. At school, I was expected to conform but always refused. All I've ever wanted to be is my odd, long-haired self rather than pretend to be something I'm not, just to fit in, even though that's meant feeling like an outcast. Especially now, after all the anguish it's brought, changing that approach isn't something I find myself willing to do. It would feel like giving in, or being dishonest. Maybe my *Körper* and *Leib* are too similar to play nicely together. Or they've both tried to get through a door at the same time and have become wedged.

This has come up in several therapy sessions: my inability (or, at least, reluctance) to modulate my behaviour in order to adapt. It can be viewed from opposing perspectives though. A therapist once said my refusal to compromise myself at school despite the pressure to become the person I was expected to be is a sign I have a strong personality, and is something I should be very proud of. Others have since speculated that my lack of self-preservation has meant I've continued to be socially isolated, learning to do everything independently by default rather than seeking to form working connections with people, and that isolation could be feeding into the DPD.

It's confusing to think that an overly strong sense of self could now be contributing to my disrupted sense of self in a roundabout way, but it's possible. We live in the age of embracing individuality and diversity, championing strong independent characters and encouraging people to be *exactly* the way they want to be without fear of judgement – and I wouldn't want that to be any different. But it's worth considering that individuality at the expense of social connections *could* run the risk of clouding our ability to know who we really are longer term. As with everything, the middle ground within the extremes is usually the healthiest place to be.

In his bestselling book about depression, *Lost Connections* (2018), journalist Johann Hari tackles this very subject. Human beings were, historically, members of tribes – and needed to be in order to survive. A single human couldn't hunt a giant animal for food, but by working together with others, we could. We needed social cohesion to evolve, and until fairly recently that continued to be the case. Now, though, in the age of smartphones, fast food and Amazon.com, we've disbanded our tribes and live largely as isolated individuals. Even sitting with our families in the evening, we don't watch the same screen anymore – we have our own. We've lost so many close personal bonds, to the corresponding detriment of our mental health. Interestingly, a community sample study in 2001 found that those who attended church had lower average levels of depersonalization, but no correlation was found with the strength of their faith, suggesting it was the social aspects that reduced dissociation (Sierra 2009). In his TED Talk of 2019, Hari notes that 'we are the loneliest society in human history' and in his book refers to research showing that lonely people's reaction times to perceiving threats are half that of socially connected people. They are 'scanning for threats because they will unconsciously know that nobody is looking out for them' (Hari 2018, p.82). Remember what we heard in the last chapter about always being on red alert and full of fight or flight anxiety keeping the DPD mechanism going?

For some, though, it can run deeper than this. Research has found that people suffering with gender dysphoria are at much higher risk of experiencing depersonalization. Whereas 1–2 per cent of adults have clinically significant DPD, and up to 7 per cent of the general adult population may have an undiagnosed dissociative disorder of some kind (Bhandari 2020), with gender dysphoria the prevalence of dissociative disorders rises to nearly 30 per cent (Colizzi, Costa and Todarello 2015). However, the intensity of the dissociative symptoms can often be reduced through hormonal treatment and gender transitioning. Zinnia Jones is a transgender researcher and activist who has written many articles regarding the link between gender dysphoria and depersonalization, and writes:

> Descriptions of depersonalization-like experiences feature prominent-ly in many trans people's recountings of their lives prior to transition, and these symptoms can heavily impact their general quality of life. But with very little attention given to depersonalization as a discrete symptom experienced by many with gender dysphoria, some trans people may struggle to recognize that this could be an indicator of

dysphoria and may not be aware that they could find relief via transitioning. (Jones 2018)

This does strongly suggest that a conflict within our sense of who we are can contribute to the onset and continuation of DPD. As gender dysphoria – defined as 'where a person experiences discomfort or distress because there's a mismatch between their biological sex and gender identity' (NHS 2020) – heightens the prevalence of dissociation, and 'resolving' the mismatch through transitioning can reduce it, I think the same could be true for other aspects of our personalities.

Dr Orna Guralnik, a New York-based psychologist and TV personality, offers a perspective on a core reason why DPD can manifest in a person that I think absolutely ties in with this ideology:

> Depersonalization often has something to do with people feeling in some way at odds with their socio-political milieu, in a way that it's hard for them to articulate. There's some kind of misfit or double-message around socio-cultural coordinates that often goes completely missed in the work with people with depersonalization, and it's super-helpful to focus on that.

Misalignments within our sense of self (e.g. being born into a certain 'class' of family, having a political or religious belief expected of you that other elements of your personality oppose, perhaps being fundamentally cisgender yet feeling at odds with what society suggests it means to be a man or a woman) can be at least partly responsible for *some* instances of depersonalization. The concept reminds me of when a working-class band writes a song about not having any money and it becomes a hit – they then have two contrasting halves of their identity. I've felt stuck in the middle in so many areas of my life and fairly opposed to a lot of things expected of me, so this is something that resonates deeply.

So, are there any more philosophical outlooks we could explore to repair the disruption in our sense of self and bring it back towards what might be considered 'normal'? It's important to stress that the vast majority of treatments for DPD (discussed in Chapter 10) are centred around psychological therapies, many of which target unhelpful thinking patterns, address issues of isolation and challenge our negative schemas. But taking a more abstract approach does throw up some interesting alternatives. In the same way that our sense of self begins to be formed through tactile interactions and other multi-sensory connections once we're born – and even before-hand – I ask Dr Ciaunica if the use of touch could be a therapeutic angle we sufferers could explore to *reconnect*. This is her reply:

I think it could play a key role, most certainly not by itself but in orchestration with other approaches. Touch is fundamental in many ways: First, it's the first sense to develop in the womb. Second, we can't switch it off. Whatever we do, we are constantly touching something. Third, and most importantly, touch has an affective, communicative dimension that is now well documented. Recent work in neuroscience has identified a specific pathway for what has been labelled 'affective touch', which is distinct from the discriminatory touch. This type of slow caress-like touch is mediated by the C Tactile afferents system and found only on the hairy skin of the body.[1] The way you *feel* is the way you are in the world - not how you understand it, but the way you are. The classic example is that you can read books about the neural and

---

1   Dr Ciaunica is referencing Löken *et al.* (2009).

motor mechanisms underlying the process of swimming, but if I throw you in the water, can you swim? Going back to the case of depersonalization: If you are driven to constantly overthink and over-scrutinize the process of swimming or living, it might prevent you from actually doing it. Similarly, if you are overwhelmed with deep existential questions such as 'Who am I?' 'What is real?' or 'What is the self?', these third-person observational stances on your experiences may disrupt the basic subjective experience of just being yourself. Paradoxically, by wanting to explore it objectively, you may alter its basic and transparent subjectivity. What is really interesting about tactile experiences is that they reveal the boundaries between the 'I' and the 'other'. By forgetting about the self and focusing on the close interaction with the 'other', one may sub-receptively get back closer to one's self.

The idea of using our bodies and touch to feel reconnected to our sense of self is an interesting one – dodie explains:

I really like it when people scratch me or twist my arms or just touch me. It puts me back in my body and makes me feel cared for.

So, it can be a reliable grounding technique for some, at least. There are also studies currently taking place at Goldsmiths, University of London, investigating the role that bodily awareness can potentially play in relieving DPD. It involves participants learning dance routines and measuring certain diagnostics before and after enacting them over a period of time. The study is still ongoing at the time of writing, so couldn't be discussed by the research team, but I'm eagerly awaiting the results.

I've always told people that the closest I ever come to feeling 'connected' to any experience is when I'm playing a guitar really effing loud. Every small movement is grossly exaggerated into hundreds of screeching decibels and – without wishing to sound too Spiñal Tap – there's a connection between the guitar and my *self* that goes beyond a cognitive one. Playing the guitar is who I am, and those lumps of wood get me as close to feeling like *me* as I'm ever able to get. I wonder if it's better able to break through the 'barrier' of depersonalization by pounding all my senses at once in brutal ways I can't ignore? The study I mentioned earlier that identified high levels of creative anxiety in performing artists with DPD also showed they 'had a stronger sense that the creative process offered a sense of transformation and that the creative experience was perceived as central to their sense of self' (Thompson and Jaque 2020, p.8). The disconnection might improve our abilities to switch off our self-judgement when creating, and give a deeper personal significance to the process.

Although I'd say I generally don't feel any significant emotional reaction to anything in life anymore, I can identify small reactions to certain pieces of music – they trigger some sort of response in my body. The pre-chorus of Pink Floyd's 'Comfortably Numb', with its descending string motifs, gives me the chills. The strained harmonies of Barber's 'Adagio for Strings' are so emotive you can't really fail to feel *something*. And when Dave Grohl is screaming 'If everything could ever feel this real forever!' at me every time I see the Foo Fighters play 'Everlong', it punches me in a bittersweet way. There's a fundamental characteristic of music that seems to communicate with us on a very primeval level, even if it's a shouty man reminding you of everything you're missing out on in life. Perhaps it bypasses our cognition, to an extent, allowing our self to interpret it. As pianist

James Rhodes (2016) put it, music is 'a language that we don't know we're all fluent in'.

We still absolutely have a sense of self – and I believe there are ways to reconnect the elements of it that might have slipped away from us. People have recovered from this nightmare and continue to do so. Research is being done into it all the time. Depersonalization doesn't fundamentally change a person. We're still *us*, deep down, although getting back to *us* won't be a quick fix – and it will definitely be an uphill struggle. But the simple act of redefining 'lost' as 'disrupted' has given me increased hope.

6.
'...But Isn't Cannabis Cool?'

Drugs and DPD

Back in February 2008, when everything at school was starting to boil over, there was a parents' evening it was mandatory to attend. I was feeling awful: beyond exhausted, drowning in coursework and earlier that day I'd endured a 20-minute assembly having hardback hymn books pitched at my head by the bullies. So, I really could have done without it.

The evening didn't exactly go as planned because, aside from my music teachers, everybody demolished me. I was depicted as a lazy underachiever who was going to flunk all my exams if I didn't get off my arse and start doing some work. In truth, I was buckling under the pressure, over-working myself and feeling so permanently under attack from everybody and everything that I couldn't think straight. In some ways they were right to question the drop in performance but couldn't have been more prejudicing as to the possible reasons why. I felt they were no better than the bullies. Everybody was out to get me that night.

After getting home, my parents went straight out with some friends, so I was on my own and feeling lower than I'd ever felt previously. This was the first time I remember drinking simply through depression and wanting to numb the pain. I went to the drinks cupboard and poured myself a huge glass of something. I think it was Jack Daniels. I didn't much care what it was. After a few of those, I gave up on the glass and sat on the sofa in the dark, chugging neat whisky from the bottle. I genuinely felt like I wanted to die.

But then I remembered: some cannabis cookies had been acquired a few days previously. I'd never tried any drug before – it's not a side of life that interests me – but with my inhibitions loosened by the industrial quantities of whisky, I decided to chow down on a cookie. I had no idea what to expect, but in my naivety, I was somewhat disappointed when I didn't feel anything within a couple of minutes. So, I ate the other four.

Before too long, I was becoming the sofa.

I don't remember feeling distressed by the experience – I don't remember much at all, to be honest. I just recall feeling like the room was spinning. I certainly didn't feel scared or panicky, just super-chilled. Eventually, I managed to haul myself upstairs, and the following morning I woke up with a banging headache and my Les Paul hidden in a wardrobe – a common occurrence whenever I was drunk, as apparently my subconscious liked to protect my best guitar from myself. I woke up, got dressed, hid the empty Jack Daniels bottle behind my bed and went to school. Within a couple of weeks, the haziness was in my mind and my decline into depersonalization had begun.

I always suspected the sudden hit of strong psychoactive chemicals might have been responsible for the way I was feeling, and as soon as I discovered depersonalization and read more about it, so many stories about 'ending up' with the condition following drug use were all over the internet. A huge number of people were talking on forums about getting 'baked' and the sensation 'never going away'. (Jane, whose story appeared in the *Guardian* newspaper article I have previously referred to [Swains 2015], also said that her depersonalization had come on after consuming cannabis.) According to one study, approximately 25 per cent of patients with DPD were found to have had the onset coincide with illicit drug use, with half of those cases being from cannabis specifically (Sierra 2009, p.66).

What had I done to myself? Had the cannabis broken my brain? What was I even doing taking something like that because I was drunk and depressed? Why didn't they cover this in health lessons at school? I'd never have taken it if I'd known this could happen. I deserved to be feeling spaced out. What an idiot.

Given how common and significant the link between DPD and recreational substances is, I wanted to dig into this further. Why is it that so many people who take drugs either experience symptoms or develop the condition? As alluded to earlier, the spacey sensations of depersonalization can very much parallel the mind-altering effect of being under the influence of some recreational drugs. Cannabis especially can make you feel zoned out, like you're floating, physically numb, and impair your cognition. So, if you're thinking you've experienced an episode of depersonalization whilst taking drugs but it went away as you came down, there's a possibility you may have 'just' been high. With hindsight, my DPD does now feel similar to what little I remember about being stoned.

Another important thing – which I'd hope would be obvious, but experience has proven otherwise – is that if you're worried about drugs causing depersonalization or making any mental health problem worse, please, stop taking the drug. I've lost count of the number of times people have emailed me with stories of being horribly distressed by episodes of depersonalization through drug use – but have then told me they'll be getting high with their mates again that evening and are 'hoping for a better experience this time'. It really isn't worth it, because it can potentially lead to worse things. As Tom told me:

> I'd had a few foreshadowings of it when I'd been stoned before in really minor doses - but then it suddenly happened in a very extreme way. I then had three years of really intense depersonalization.

Abstaining from drugs is a fairly simple solution to a logical problem when it's being done socially rather than through addiction – as marijuana *usually* is. It worries me when people comment on my short film and *DPD Diaries* videos with stories of depersonalization ruining their life, but their avatar is a giant cannabis leaf.

Are the psychoactive chemicals in these substances playing havoc with our brain chemistry? Are they reprogramming us to dissociate? I asked Dr Hunter about the link and she had a very interesting take on why it exists.

> I think any substances are red herrings. Yes, you can have an 'unreal' experience that can then be more easily triggered again, but I don't believe it's a physical or permanent reaction to the drug itself. I think it's the reaction to the experiences people have on the drug. When you drill into it, person after person...from the experiences of being under the influence of whatever it is, they start to feel really panicky. So, it's the 'bad trip' situation ... Some people have taken it for a long period of time with no adversity. If it's the first time, they have no comparison, but if they've taken it a lot and it's been fine - no adverse effects - but then they

> take it and end up with depersonalization, I think that often there
> might be other things going on in their life, or they had a bad
> reaction that particular time they were taking it. Maybe they took
> a combination of drugs, or more of it.

This wasn't entirely what I was expecting to hear but, on reflection, it makes perfect sense. With depersonalization being a 'protective reflex', our mind might feel the need to protect us from the effects of the drug. Especially if it's a drug we haven't taken before, or we've had a higher dose than we're used to, the resulting trip is going to be a new experience and one that's likely to be quite frightening as our brain has its cognitions manipulated in ways we can't control.

The feeling of spiralling out of control can cause us to panic, or at least experience significant anxiety, which then acts as another stressor to feed into any potential psychological overload. As before, if our cognitive load is already high, a bad drug trip can cause a big spike that blows the fuses. Our mind becomes suddenly overwhelmed and, out of self-preservation, dissociates to protect us from the anxiety. If the trip is especially traumatic (as the hallucinogenic trips brought on by magic mushrooms and LSD often can be), even without too many pre-existing stressors the sudden barrage of terror might be like the fuses being hit by a bolt of lightning – they'll blow regardless.

This very much ties in with how Jane describes her cannabis experience when she was 18 (when her depersonalization first began):

> I'd smoked before and didn't particularly enjoy it. I got quite pan-
> icky, but it peaked and left me quite quickly. Then, I took cannabis
> again a few months later. I ate it in a yoghurt, so it lasted in my
> body a bit longer. Having taken the first lot, nothing happened,
> so I took a second lot – but as soon as I did, the first lot kicked in.

> Two things happened: one, it was like I 'zoomed back' in my per-spective; and two, it was like my gaze fixated on things and there was a delay moving from one thing to another. I now understand that the feeling triggered a panic attack and, as I panicked, that feeling became more intense. Added to that, the second dose of cannabis was kicking in, which made me panic even more, and I went into a cycle of what I would call 'catastrophic panic'. I was crying, begging for help, drinking water, eating things. I tried to sleep but every time I lay down, I felt like I was tumbling into a black hole. I woke up the next morning and it was a bit better in that I wasn't completely 'zoomed out', but I felt I couldn't think... There was a 'processing gap'. The concepts of viewing and understanding the world, reacting to it and processing that reaction – they all seemed to be separate acts rather than happening smoothly. In a way it felt like I was paralytically drunk. The process of consciousness felt very 'clunky'.

The theory fits Jane's situation then. The cannabis almost certainly didn't cause a chemical change in her brain as she'd taken it before with no lasting ill-effects. Even at low doses, it had made her feel panicky. When she took the higher dose (or two), the severity of the trip was much worse, and the feeling of being out of control caused a huge panic attack. It was likely *that* reaction to the drug – the panic – which triggered the depersonalization. Professor David has a similar perspective:

> The idea of a trigger (in a susceptible individual) is easy to accept. But whether it is a 'cause' is more difficult. Our work[1] suggests

---

1   One such study is Medford *et al.* 2003.

that the kind of symptoms people describe in depersonalization that followed cannabis, compared with depersonalization arising out of the blue, are the same. This suggests to us that many different things can push someone down the path towards depersonalization, but the path takes you to the same point. Whether chemicals within cannabis can 'poison the brain' in a permanent or semi-permanent way is unknown.

Interestingly, some people have found CBD (cannabidiol) oil helps to relieve symptoms of depersonalization – essentially, it's cannabis with the psychoactive compound (THC) removed, so it doesn't make you 'high'. It's a fairly new experimental treatment that's come about following pushes for the legalization of cannabis in healthcare, but reading around on forums, some sufferers do say they've had positive results. It's said to help anxiety and depression, so I suspect CBD may have mostly had an effect on those with transient depersonalization stemming from those two areas. I tried it for a few months and found it not to have any benefit. This does suggest further that the cannabis itself isn't what is 'causing' depersonalization through chemical means, as CBD oil – at least the one I took – is 'pure' cannabis (just without the THC). It should be noted that frequent cannabis usage – especially potent strains ('skunk') – has been strongly linked to other mental health conditions, such as psychosis (Davis 2019).

Just as panic can be a self-perpetuating cycle (the fear of having a panic attack directly causing another one), this can also be true with drugs. The experience of a bad trip can be so terrifying that we then live in fear of having that experience again. It's a 'panic cycle', of sorts. Taking the drug again, even in a smaller dose or just thinking about what happened, might bring about that anxiety. With the sensory nature of the amygdala, simply smelling a waft of someone's cigarette smoke might set off that association. It's a loose analogy, but there are certain alcoholic drinks I now can't touch even though I previously loved them – for example, just the smell of Jägermeister can make me retch nowadays after making my way through two litres of it one night and suffering the consequences.

In the last decade, various states in America have begun to legalize cannabis – occasionally just for medicinal purposes, but mostly for recreation. As far as I'm aware, nobody is monitoring this specifically, but it would be interesting to know whether cases of DPD – or even just mental health problems in general – have risen in those states since the legislation has been brought in. My Dutch friend Michelle has always told me that cannabis use in Holland is fairly low amongst nationals – it's typically tourists who exploit the legality. This makes me think that having it available in previously 'dry' states will mean people go somewhat overboard (until the novelty factor wears off) and the prevalence of drug-related mental health problems could increase. Canada legalized cannabis in 2018, and although figures aren't yet publicly available, experts have predicted a sharp increase in cannabis-induced psychosis as a result (O'Brien 2019).

All of this raises an important question about my particular case. If the drug-trigger trend exists because of anxiety caused by the psychological effects of feeling out of control rather than the chemicals themselves, why did the onset of my DPD coincide with the cannabis cookie incident? After all, from what I remember, I didn't panic. I felt dizzy and wanted to listen to jazz, but that was about it. If I didn't have any adverse psychological reaction, did the cannabis even trigger my DPD?

The truth is – it probably didn't. More than a decade down the line nobody can say that for certain, but it's likely not related in any way. The DPD didn't come on during or immediately after the trip and I didn't get any obvious anxiety from the experience. It was a good few weeks before I started to feel hazy. In addition, DPD onsets with a drug-trigger component are generally quite sudden and extreme, whereas mine came from almost insignificant beginnings and was a slow decline over many years. With everything going on at school at that time, I was so overwhelmed that the torture of the parents' evening was likely more of a factor than the weed. I was probably close to the point of DPD setting in anyway.

After many years thinking I'd fried my brain with a dose of bad drugs, I was *likely* barking up the wrong tree. I know it wasn't a wise thing to do – and is absolutely not something I'd suggest trying – but I did take cannabis again many years later in an Amsterdam *koffieshop* purely to see if it affected my depersonalization. It didn't.

7.
Seeking Initial Help and Being in Therapy

With the average diagnosis time dancing around the decade mark, it's no surprise that in a worrying number of situations medical professionals haven't heard of DPD. Dr Guralnik says:

> There are not many people who study this or focus on it in their work, which is frankly totally bizarre to me because it's so common. I don't really understand why people aren't specializing in it, or studying it, or taking it more as a point of focus.

Sadly, it's usually down to people with lived experience to become the *de facto* experts and drive the treatment process.

One of my earliest memories of the mental health services was on the Isle of Wight around 2011. I walked in, not really knowing what to expect, and was asked to take a seat in the small waiting room. There were three other people already in there, all of whom appeared very visibly and severely depressed. As I sat down and picked up the customary copy of *Autocar* magazine, I noticed they were piping in the local radio station, which was playing Radiohead. I looked around again at the trio of long faces staring at their shoes. 'Karma Police' wasn't helping anybody in there.

We'll be looking at the specific treatments typically used by DPD specialists in Chapter 10, but just knowing where to turn in the first instance when you're struggling can be a significant hurdle in itself. Fairly early on in your journey, you'll likely end up in some form of psychological therapy within your local area – maybe DPD-specific but probably more generalized (I've been through so many different ones over the years). The thought of opening up about your problems to a near-stranger is something most people really aren't comfortable about doing at first. I know I wasn't in the early days, although I feel very used to it now. The idea of running a YouTube channel discussing my struggles isn't something I'd have dreamed of doing pre-therapy.

The provision of healthcare varies from one country to the next, which will have a significant bearing on people's abilities to access help. The UK has the National Health Service (NHS), which entitles any UK citizen to free healthcare at the state's expense. For mental health especially though, wait times can be fairly lengthy, so private healthcare runs alongside it for those willing and able to foot the bill themselves. The system in Canada is fairly similar. Germany requires all citizens to have health insurance by law. Australia works more on a subsidy system but prioritizes mental health. Gerald, a sufferer from Sydney, explains:

> It's not free at the point of service ... but the state funds 50–60 per cent of all care. In the case of mental health, they have a specific 'Mental Healthcare Plan'. So, you go to your GP, and they might refer you to a psychologist ... There's not a long wait time, and you

get six sessions completely free. But if you still need assistance after that, you go back to your GP, they do another plan, and it's entirely free again - and this can go on for years. When you get into 'full' psychiatric medicine (being sectioned, psychosis, schizophrenia, etc.) you can apply to the state and get a 'Disability Support Pension' - if a psychiatrist deems you unfit to work, the state pays you welfare for rent, food, etc. If you qualify for that, you're very well taken care of - mental healthcare in Australia is very good.

One problem case that has come up many times researching this book, though, is America. Accessing any healthcare there can be a big problem. A friend of mine road-tripped Route 66 a few years back and met people who had stitched up their own injuries with a needle and thread because they couldn't afford to go to the hospital. Dr Guralnik adds:

This is just my own political opinion - but the US healthcare system is a broken system. It's a very expensive system that doesn't provide much, and a lot of the money goes towards the various bureaucratic systems that manage the healthcare, not to the providers. It's pretty horrific. Some people are insured but they're limited to [consultations with] people who are on insurance panels - and those are typically people that are either younger in their career and not specialized, or people who are on the margins of the work. There's no way you can see somebody who specializes in depersonalization through the healthcare system.

There can be cultural reasons for not being able to access help, too. A sufferer from Zambia told me:

> Seeing a psychologist or psychiatrist is almost impossible here. You need to have a lot of courage to access such services because of the stigma attached to going to a mental hospital. People around you might think you are insane the moment you talk about visiting [one].

Even in the USA, not accessing help can be cultural – Jenny explains:

> One of the key American tendencies that has routinely fucked us over is this idea of 'pulling yourself up by your own bootstraps': working harder and overcoming things by yourself without needing assistance. American exceptionalism and things like that ... The idea of 'just asking for help' is anathema to a lot of people's views of themselves. There's a relentless positivity to Americans – there's a bit of phoniness in that.

You do need a good amount of self-confidence when talking to clinicians who might not be aware of DPD, as in my experience many haven't been sympathetic. You have to be politely persistent, and unaccepting of being fobbed off. Short of seeing a specialist, I've personally found neuropsychiatrists to usually be the most knowledgeable about DPD. Just giving a name to the symptoms can reduce anxiety around them. As Jane puts it:

> It gave me a search term to Google and verify that it was exactly what I was experiencing. I had a name. I knew what it was. I suddenly didn't feel like a freak anymore. It validated the experience.

As important as it is to learn about depersonalization yourself – and you'll need a good personal knowledge of the condition going forwards – there really isn't any substitute for seeking professional medical help in the first instance, even if that's just to get you into the system. Before seeking a formal diagnosis, accessing support on a local level can be helpful to stop us sinking further. There can be a colossal amount of sitting around and waiting for things to happen when trying to access specialist help, especially in overstretched public health services, so anything that can help to prop you up in the meantime is worth exploring.

Approaching your doctor is probably the most sensible place to start, because they are the ones best placed to refer you onwards. The chances are you'll be met with a blank expression when you mention symptoms of depersonalization, let alone DPD, so I've sometimes found it helpful to take some paperwork along to appointments. You'll only have a limited time with them, so arriving armed with reasonable information and an action plan of what you'd like them to do can be sensible to get the most out of an appointment. It's best to take literature from a medically recognized source rather than printouts from public forums – the entry on DPD in the *British Medical Journal* generally carries a lot of weight with professionals around the world (and is available on the Unreal charity website).

At this point, it might be worthwhile to ask whether there are any tests they could run to rule out the symptoms being caused by anything physical in the brain – as before, that's statistically rare in DPD, but if tests are available it might make sense to have them if it's something worrying you. The MRI and EEG scans I had early on eliminated the possibility of me having a brain tumour or any other physical abnormality, which was definitely a comfort. I've also had many blood tests along the way, for everything from nutritional deficiencies to diabetes and hormone imbalances. They've all come back with no significant results, but eliminating anything can both reassure us and narrow the search field going forward.

Doctors sometimes try to prescribe you antidepressants – which may or may not be appropriate for your specific case – but accessing psychological therapies is what I would be pushing for, meds or no meds. For me, primary care (the 'entry-level' mental health services – which I don't mean to sound demeaning) has only been able to offer a CBT-based approach to anxiety and low mood. Although this might not be ideally suited to tackling DPD specifically, it can have a positive effect for some – I know people who have gained benefit from being helped to manage their anxiety, for example.

Another area of potential support thrown up by a Google search is the abundance of online depersonalization-centric groups and forums. There are some on Facebook (advocate and author Jeffrey Abugel runs a US-based non-profit called Initiative for Depersonalization Studies). There's also a thriving community over at dpselfhelp.com, as well as a /dprd subsection of Reddit, to name but a few. These can be great places to learn about the condition from the experiences of fellow sufferers and ask for their advice. Alina tells me:

> We discuss how to approach mental health professionals about DPD, how to describe what we are feeling more accurately, and how to navigate the system to get quicker access to treatment.

However, I would offer a word of caution about these places: discussions can get very dark. DPD is a living nightmare and we naturally seek an outlet for our intense frustrations – especially when engaging with those who know *exactly* what we're going through. In my time visiting them, I found exposing myself to thread after thread of other people's suffering didn't help my own mental health one bit. I don't mean that to sound heartless, but you can't take on somebody else's problems to the detriment of yourself – that's the first rule of peer support. Definitely check out these websites as they're packed with useful and interesting chat but be sure to look after yourself first and foremost. If it's not the right time to be looking at them, leave them for later. They're also not for everybody, depending on how sensitive you are to potential triggers.

Going through a publicly funded healthcare model as I have for many years, there's always been a level system – a bit like a computer game – and only once you've exhausted all options on one tier do you get to progress to the next. I had to spend so many hours swimming in circles in primary care before managing to progress to the experts. I lost track of the amount of times I explained my symptoms to somebody, only to be given advice like 'Have you considered taking a nice hot bath?' Unsurprisingly, I was sceptical of chronic dissociation being suddenly helped by warm water and a capful of bubble bath. Similarly, one health professional told Alina to 'maybe just try to ignore it' and another sufferer was advised to 'put your feet up with a cup of tea'.

Making it through any mental health appointment can be draining and upsetting, even without dismissal and trivialization. Comments like the ones above coming from the very people holding the keys to the next stage of our treatment are especially difficult to hear as you know they're not going to be opening doors for you any time soon. Within public healthcare though, you're absolutely entitled to seek a second opinion from another professional and can appeal the outcome of meetings deciding where to send you next. Patronizing clinicians are frustrating as hell to come up against, but you can always ask governing bodies to escalate your case if you feel they haven't properly dealt with the problem. I was once sarcastically told, 'So, you feel a bit "spaced out", do you? You know, it's very normal to feel spaced out sometimes. I think you're maybe just a little bit tired. Dehydration can make us feel wobbly – do you drink any water? Why don't you try thinking about happy things?' and as soon as the session was over, I requested to never have to deal with that clinician again. If you're paying a professional privately who treats you like this, I'd suggest quickly cutting your losses and finding another who's more likely to take you seriously.

It's also relevant to ask yourself whether you need to find an in-person therapist at all. There are a number of online DPD 'programmes' you can purchase – can you just pay the money and go through one of those? Well, you can – but, again, I would offer a few words of caution. As we'll discuss shortly, although there's a framework that depersonalization-centric therapists will often start with, the overall treatment plan – especially for chronic, long-term DPD – ultimately needs to be bespoke to the individual. There cannot be a 'one approach fixes all' mentality. Through asking around, and having bought one myself once upon a time, I'd say those programmes usually seem to be a recounting of what the author's personal treatment was, as well as more generalized techniques for relaxation and controlling anxiety, which is fine – it means they'll likely benefit a good amount of people. However, where I'd disagree with how some of them are marketed is that they repeatedly use the word 'cure' and lead people to believe that through spending the money, you will be 'cured'. I don't doubt that the authors (many of whom have no medical training) overcame *their* depersonalization using the techniques they discuss – probably under the care of trained medical professionals – but that's the only thing that can really be said with certainty. It needs to be stressed there are no guarantees of your own personal recovery, and any website that tries to promise you that for a price is hyperbole at best. I'd go out on a limb and suggest they're better suited to people suffering with transient episodes of depersonalization, as those patients are often more responsive to generalized techniques. Please do try one of these programmes if you feel it might help, but as somebody who once bought one out of desperation and found it not to be the silver bullet it claimed to be, it is worth managing your expectations. Recovery is a fundamentally different concept to a 'cure', too –as we'll discuss in Chapter 10.

There's also self-help literature written directly by clinicians – the *Overcoming Depersonalization and Feelings of Unreality* book by Baker *et al.* (2010) is one such example. In it, they discuss clinical information and offer CBT-based self-help techniques derived from the basic framework they use in practice. Dr Daphne Simeon and Jeffrey Abugel's book *Feeling Unreal: Depersonalization Disorder and the Loss of the Self* (2006) also comes highly recommended by many. If you're wanting to try tackling your problems yourself before seeking individual professional help – as well as learning about DPD – I'd personally start with the self-help material written directly by the experts.

After a decade's experience of it, I'd describe psychological therapy (in its many forms) as being eye-opening and revelationary at best, and a hot coal suppository at worst. You're not there for a jolly; you're there to pull your personality and experiences apart and look for answers in difficult places. It's far from an easy process. Memories and painful incidents need to be analysed and processed. Once you get into the habit of doing this in your head, it's hard to switch it off, which is partly the point. As it was once put to me, 'We don't want you to be in therapy forever. We need you to be your own therapist.'

I'll give you a quick example of something therapy threw up for me. It's difficult to talk about as it's indicative of a major flaw in my character, but I'll trust you with it. In 2015, I contracted an evil virus that attacked my heart and put me in intensive care. I had to be taken for scans in a wheelchair with a defibrillator attached in case I conked out, and was told survival wasn't guaranteed. But those ten days were some of the most contented days of my entire life. I knew there was a chance I might die, but that didn't bother me in the slightest. I felt the closest to happiness I've felt since having DPD and, arguably, ever. When I was discharged, I don't think I've ever felt more desperately depressed. As soon as I was going to be okay, I wanted to die.

Shouldn't the emotions have been the other way around? Therapy helped me to see that my happiness was probably down to suddenly feeling valued by the people I was surrounded by. Doctors would come and speak to me and have my best interests at heart – no pun intended – without any hidden agenda or wishing to belittle me. I had a lovely (and slightly gorgeous) Irish nurse who would sit and talk to me about music and growing up in Dublin, and I didn't even care that she was using me as a pincushion. Once I was discharged and came out of that bubble, I crashed back into my real life. Through analysing this, I now understand that many of my actions are fundamentally driven by a desire to be liked and accepted by other people following years of rejection. That was hard to hear. But it's a decent example of the sort of bombshell that can come out of sessions, whether you're wanting them to or not. Therapy can hurt – you just have to believe it's for a greater good.

If you're having sessions, or starting them soon, the advice I would offer is to go into them being as prepared as you can. You're usually given homework that forms the basis of the next session. If you have to keep a diary (be that a 'traditional' one, a thought diary, a food diary, etc.), do it thoroughly and keep all of your paperwork ordered in a file. Read last week's notes before you go into your current session, to revise them and avoid repeating yourself. Some therapists encourage you to record your sessions – if that's the case, or if you're allowed to do it, listen back to the previous session on the day of your next. Make notes of things you want to ask about. You only get a limited time with your therapist, so make it count.

That said, a trend that does seem to have emerged (perhaps this is indicative of how training guidelines might have changed over time, as it's usually been younger therapists I've had where this has happened) is that the patient is encouraged to 'drive the sessions'. I think there's a lot of benefit to this approach. If anything is going to make somebody switch off, it'll be a dictatorial therapist. But there needs to be a working balance here as the onus can't be solely on the patient to formulate the therapy structure. At times it's felt like that for me and I've found myself feeling very annoyed when I've sat down in sessions only to be asked, yet again, 'So, what would you like to cover today?', when the answer is, fairly obviously, 'I want to cover what you, as the trained professional, deem most appropriate for me, the patient, who's struggling and knows squat all about psychology.' If this happens, I'd urge you to raise it with your therapist. Explain that you're feeling lost and would appreciate their guidance in structuring the sessions, otherwise you risk them being a waste of time. We obviously don't *want* to discuss difficult memories at length. Sometimes a professional nudge in that direction is absolutely necessary to avoid skirting around major problems.

No therapy I've ever had has been able to improve my symptoms, but that's not to say I haven't gotten benefit from them. For example. I now understand events from my past and people in my life far more than I used to. I've managed to reduce the frequency of my headaches by discovering (through keeping an hourly diary for a few weeks) that it wasn't just overexertion and tiredness that would cause them – whenever I was working flat out on something or travelling around, I would forget to eat, and the following day I'd invariably crash and burn as my blood sugar fell through the floor.

To live with long-term DPD, we're forced to evolve a sort of psychological endurance that keeps us afloat even when – in a life sense – we might be being forced to just tread water. I consider myself mentally strong in many ways, because after over a decade of feeling like I have all the future prospects of a padlock on an episode of *Storage Hunters*,[1] and getting progressively stronger thoughts to let go, I'm still here and still pushing forwards in the ways I can. But despite this, one thing I've struggled with so much is the lack of ongoing support following various treatments.

Being in therapy does help you to feel like you're making progress – simply by virtue of doing *something*, if nothing else. But like the psychiatrist who discharged me because I wouldn't take their anti-psychotic drugs, it's become common for courses of treatment to end with nothing more than a farewell handshake and good wishes, rather than there being any form of an ongoing support network put in place. Therapy might feel like you're heading in the right direction, but finishing it with no improvements to write home about has then been made *so* much harder by being left absolutely on my own with the ball firmly in my court to figure out my next move. I pride myself on being forward thinking and determined when it comes to accessing help – and I research DPD far more than is probably healthy – but I'm not an expert. I don't know whether I should now be looking for a new medication, booking a different trauma therapy or joining a gardening group. I need somebody who's qualified to know what they're on about to help me figure that out. Treatments seem to largely be viewed as absolutes rather than a link in a chain.

The amount of waiting around is inevitable to some extent, given

---

1   Reality TV show in which contestants bid to purchase the contents of abandoned storage lockers. Each segment typically begins with a security guard chopping a padlock to reveal the goods.

how overstretched many health services are, but extended periods of nothing are another area where lack of support has been a nightmare. In May 2017 I saw a psychiatrist to ask for a referral to the Maudsley Hospital – it took them five months to write the letter, despite me chasing their secretary on a fortnightly basis. *Five months.* Once I was assessed at the Maudsley, the waiting list to begin therapy was almost a year.[2] After eight weeks, extra funding had to be applied for to have additional sessions, resulting in a gap of nearly four months. During these long periods of sitting around and waiting for a phone call, I can honestly tell you that my mental health deteriorated badly – I was keeping myself as busy and productive as I could, but nevertheless many months would pass with no updates, no indication of when anything might happen and no steps forward being made. It was very difficult to deal with. I felt forgotten about.

My best advice to anybody going through any sort of referral process is this: you need to be your own secretary. In a perfect world, medical machines should just *work*, but often we need to be the ones driving things forward. If you're waiting for a letter to be sent, find out who is responsible, and within reason keep the pressure on. There's no harm in calling them up periodically and enquiring as to what progress has been made. If you're waiting on the decision of a funding meeting, find out when that meeting is and offer to provide additional information to the person chairing it – it'll probably not be required, or wanted, but at least it'll show you're serious about

---

2   The waiting list at the Maudsley is ever-changing. With only two therapists working part-time within the service (at the time of writing), it inevitably has to be a one-out-one-in arrangement. The wait time is constantly fluctuating, depending on how many people are landing on the waiting list versus the number of patients being discharged. All I can say with any certainty is that I got on the list in January 2018 and began therapy in November that year – so the wait was almost one year for me. It may be very different now.

wanting to get on with things and you'll stick in their minds. If you're going into an assessment for a particular purpose (such as getting an onward referral), I've sometimes found it helpful to post them some paperwork about DPD in advance (more so than I'd take along to the doctor). You'll need to be careful with this, as the last thing you want to do is offend somebody by suggesting that they won't know how to do their job, but the couple of times I've done it, the clinician has commented that it's been helpful for them – and ultimately, I've gotten what I needed.

8.
Coping Strategies for a Depersonalized Life

There's no getting around it: any long-term mental health condition is going to impact your life for the worse. You might not be able to do all the things you want to do anymore, people might not understand what you're going through and there'll be times you feel intensely frustrated by the way things are. Adapting to life with DPD has been the most excruciating thing I've ever had to do. Although my core personality hasn't really changed, I do think I've had to adopt a very different outlook to the one I once had. I've had to make changes – both on my own and under the guidance of therapists – to make things more tolerable and stop my mental health from deteriorating further.

The phrase 'coping strategy' often has negative connotations, but it shouldn't. Of course, there *are* definitely negative ones (no matter how bad you feel, you won't find any answers at the bottom of a bottle of vodka... I've looked), but accommodating any illness is in many ways a process of developing a series of positive coping mechanisms. As Merrick Pope, a Scottish self-harm nurse specialist, said in a 2020 TV documentary:

Generally, we aren't very good at looking after ourselves and coping in ways that are healthy. So, we don't phone our counsellor, have a massage and eat an organic salad when we've had a rubbishy day. We eat chips, we pick a fight with our partner, smoke fags ... It [self-harm] is culturally acceptable at different points.

When getting 300 expensive vinyl records pressed went pear-shaped (very literally), I went on a sugar binge and felt horrendous for days afterwards. Sometimes when I couldn't face going home to my ex for an evening of being shouted at, I'd go to the pub, numb everything with a few of the strongest ciders they had and say I'd missed the bus. I think most of us have felt depressed and bought something we can't afford, thinking it will somehow fix everything. I did that with a guitar last year and still feel ashamed when the finance deal nukes my bank account each month.

Behaviour like this is mostly okay for a day or two, occasionally. But avoiding these more self-destructive acts becoming our default way of coping and trying to change our thoughts and actions into healthier, more helpful ones are fairly central principles behind CBT. We'll be looking at the specific therapies for DPD and how they target the factors keeping the feedback loop going in Chapter 10. But for now, just know that many of the tactics I discuss here have been realized partially in conjunction with therapists.

It needs to be emphasized that – as always – there are no hard and fast rules to this. We're all fundamentally different and the ways we adapt ourselves to cope with adversity are a very personal thing. What will drastically improve the life of one person could initiate a downward spiral for the next. So, take this chapter with a big pinch of salt and perhaps use it as a *starting point* to develop strategies that work for you.

The single most important thing I've found of benefit to my personal headspace has been having direction for treatment. The days of the head thing were torturous because I didn't know what was wrong and had no idea what to do – and nor did any doctor. As soon as I 'discovered' DPD, it gave me so much hope – and by reading this book, you're already miles further down that road than I was back then. Knowing I have a date in the diary for my next treatment session has been a big thing – as I said about therapy earlier, simply doing *something* can make you feel less like you're cartwheeling off into the depths of space. At the time of writing I have nothing lined up in terms of future treatment options and I feel more lost now than I have in a good while.

The major principle behind a huge amount of CBT I've had has been avoiding *rumination*: constantly worrying about how we're feeling and obsessively examining the symptoms. Dr Hallett explains:

> If you look at the dictionary definition of 'rumination', it makes reference to the action of cows 'chewing the cud'. This visual image of cows standing in a field chewing on their partly digested food over and over again I think is a useful metaphor for rumination (that is, the mental habit of going over and over past events in our mind, without moving on from them). Rumination as a thinking style is common in many different mental health conditions, including DPD. It can become particularly problematic when it prevents individuals from coming up with solutions to their problems and generating alternative perspectives or interrupts some aspect of their day-to-day life (e.g. sleeping, socialising or generally taking steps towards their goals).

Rumination is tempting, because adversities always want to be at the forefront of our minds. When we're having a particularly dire day and feel we're not able to do anything, we're left on our own with our thoughts...and as comedian Marc Maron once quipped, 'I tend towards darkness in my amateur psychoanalytic practice' (2014, p.41). The last thing we want is to be constantly 'locked on' to the sensations, monitoring them like you might a fever with a thermometer. CBT can be great for identifying exacerbating lifestyle factors too – many people find their depersonalization gets worse after drinking coffee or alcohol, for example. I've never personally found either to have a negative effect, but being aware of things that do, and taking steps to reduce them, is helpful.

I'm far from being a shining example of this myself – the share prices in Cadbury's chocolate attest to that – but eating well and trying to stay physically healthy are both very important. I find I consume crap largely through boredom. If I'm busy, I'll generally eat okay. If I'm sitting around with nothing much to do, my face is in the ice cream. A lot of people have told me they find exercise to be very helpful, not just for physical health but for the endorphin release and something else to stop them overthinking. Some have even said intense exercise has improved their depersonalization symptoms specifically. Again, I've never found it made much difference to me, nor am I a particularly athletic blob of a human anyway. But it goes without saying that good physical health should always be a priority.

Where I *have* found being active to be beneficial, though, is to do with sleep. My body clock generally feels like it's a good few hours further into any given day than it actually is – plus, I'm a fairly light sleeper to boot. I think it's important to go to bed feeling tired. This might sound obvious, but lying awake is one of the worst times for rumination and intrusive thoughts. Burning calories can help us maintain a natural sleep pattern and aid dropping off once the lights are out. Anything that helps with that is worth trying – a lot of sufferers use nighttime baths, essential oils and massages to help them wind down.

It's generally accepted that continuing to do your normal everyday things as much as possible is the healthiest way forward with DPD. There will be compromises, of course, but there's little worth in reflexively throwing in the towel on everything if you can avoid it. If you're working a job, carry on with it if you can – commitments with regular hours can be great for giving us structure and routine, as well as bringing obvious financial benefits. It might be a good idea to discuss your challenges with your employer and see if they're able to support you with kinder shift patterns, assistance with certain tasks, reassigning roles, etc. That said, DPD might have more of a bearing, depending on your occupation – if you're an airline pilot, even though DPD can be imperceptible to the outside world, it's probably not wise to be responsible for hundreds of lives every day.

Stressful jobs full of uncertainty can absolutely impact our mental health. We heard how dodie's success caused her a huge amount of overwhelm, and Jenny feels that the unpredictability of her writing work has had an impact:

> It has, in terms of the fact there's so much rejection and heartbreak in having this career - and there's very little stability, which I think is a very good counterbalance to feeling like things are derealized. The best thing for my mental health is a steady schedule: to wake up every day, go to a workout class, eat the right things and go to bed at a normal time ... but that's hard under normal circumstances. [Having] a job where every day is a little bit different and [I'm] working from home means I have to babysit myself more than other people do, I think. For my job,

it's hard because I have to really enforce some sort of schedule or sense of stability - more than if I had some sort of desk job.

Setting routines for ourselves can be very useful. Your entire week doesn't need to be diarized, but a basic framework can help. Every morning, I try to be up by 7:30am. I make sure I eat breakfast (something I'd often forget to do) and always get changed out of my pyjamas. This gets me into the headspace of 'doing' rather than lounging around. I'll sit at my desk, reply to important emails and write a list of things that need to be done that day. I'll divide them into categories: 'Essentials', 'If I Have Time' and 'For Me'. I try to have at least two things in that last category to motivate me and take my mind off the more mundane jobs - I don't *need* to drive to Antonio's and get a takeout pizza, but holy hell do I look forward to it. Before I turn the lights out at night, I spend ten minutes playing guitar - not plugged in, just sat on my bed quietly - because I find it clears my mind. I don't try to learn anything new or play anything difficult - that time is purely for relaxation. Building time into our day to relax is something that seems to be ever harder to do nowadays.

The likes of meditation, mindfulness, grounding techniques and yoga can be useful practices to help 'put us back in our bodies' and many have told me the benefit for them has been substantial. Jen explains:

Simple breathing practices can be really helpful for grounding, as can subtle movements. When things are really bad, I try and get my logical brain working, telling myself what I can see and describing in detail what I can hear, taste, smell, etc.

Many favour the '5,4,3,2,1' technique of focusing on your various senses.[1] However, it should also be noted that some find the likes of meditation to have the opposite effect – being on your own with your thoughts isn't always the best thing. As ever, it depends on what sort of person you are as to what works.

During my therapy at the Maudsley, I spent a few weeks keeping a diary of everything I was doing and grading how much I felt I was struggling. What we noticed was there are definitely times I find tougher than others, even though my DPD symptoms are pretty constant. This is what first introduced me to the idea of *cognitive loading* (essentially, the 'layering up' of different stressors we talked about with Dr Hunter earlier in Chapter 4). Dr Hallett describes the concept:

> Our working memory is where we do our information processing and it's limited in its capacity and duration. A heavy cognitive load can have a negative impact on an individual's ability to complete a task and can impede a person's ability to learn new information.

My capacity to cope with each day seems pretty maxed out by the DPD, so if I then have to deal with tiredness, stress, arguments, a heavy workload, etc., it makes certain times much more trying. I've tried to take steps to reduce those other stressors and avoid unnecessarily difficult situations when I can. It hasn't helped the DPD, but it has reduced the boom and bust cycle that would make certain periods trickier for me.

One of the most reliable ways I've found to keep myself occupied is indulging my hobbies. By definition, they're things we want to do

---

1   In this common grounding technique you try to focus your senses by identifying five things you can see, four things you can touch, three things you can hear, two things you can smell and one thing you can taste (or a variation on this theme).

– even though that want can be dulled. Plus, I also think keeping an 'end goal' in sight is of paramount importance to motivate us in our recovery. I'm still very driven towards being able to support myself as a professional musician, and if the circumstances ever allow it, I'll try to hit the ground running. I don't want to be starting in the same position I was when I was 18. I want the benefit of years of study and additional skills. So, although music is still a 'hobby' that keeps me distracted, I'm always trying to get better and learn new things that I can hopefully take better advantage of one day. Again, though, we need to be careful not to go too far – I easily become obsessed with things, and that can have a detrimental effect on mental health too. With many of us being creatives, using art as a coping mechanism can certainly be cathartic, but doing so publicly can have its drawbacks, as dodie has discovered:

> There's been gossipy people online making this narrative of 'dodie romanticizes mental health' because I sing about it, talk about it, etc. That's just so hard because it's like, 'Please don't take away the thing I need to get through this.'

Some find photography is a helpful tool to help them keep track of things they've been doing. Jen explains:

> I find it really useful to take pictures – almost as evidence that I've been doing or did do something, especially if I am on my own and do not have anyone to offer assurance that yes, I did do that. I often take photos of places I go to, or things that I've done ... I can look back at them with a sense of recognition.

'Logging' our movements with pictorial evidence to help us retrospectively relate to them is easy nowadays with smartphones, so it's definitely worth a try. I've always enjoyed photography and it's genuinely useful to be able to keep a visual diary, of sorts.

It's also been important to me to get outdoors as much as possible. The temptation when we're feeling bad might be to stay in bed or sit and watch television, but fresh air and sunlight really boost my mood. I've always liked nature, so going for walks in pretty places is something I try to do whenever the weather is decent. Last year, my partner also helped me to develop the small balcony area outside my bedroom that had sat unused for years. We laid some tiles, renovated an old bench and sourced loads of pots to grow some nice bee-friendly flowers. Much of this book has been written sat outside, watching my busy bees go about their business.

When it comes to adapting our lives to accommodate the condition, there are a lot of real-world grey areas for which there's simply no guidance. For example, I've sat in so many medical professionals' offices, explaining to them that I feel like I'm still asleep and dreaming. Not *once* has anybody questioned whether I should be driving a car. My take on this – aside from saying that if you don't feel safe driving, you shouldn't drive – is that it's another of those things where I've had to separate what I feel from what I know to be true. I *feel* I shouldn't be able to do it, yet I *know* I'm able to, and I've not had a single accident in 13 years. My reactions are fine. Some people have written to me saying they've just had a birthday and their parents are expecting them to start driving lessons, but they're scared to do so, which I guess makes things more problematic. I enjoy go-karting and you need quick reactions for that, else you're eating tyre wall for dinner. If you're questioning your abilities behind the wheel, karting can be a fun way to test them out in a controlled environment.

Another hazy area is travel insurance. Do you need to declare

DPD when you go abroad, even though they definitely won't have heard of it? Or a more delicate issue: does DPD 'class' as a disability? Gerald told us that Australia is good at supporting those who are struggling mentally, but assessment guidelines for mental health conditions are often vague. My worry, having spoken to several sufferers who've had varying degrees of success in claiming state benefits, is that it might depend on how sympathetic a particular assessor is, and also on the patient's ability to argue their case. This would make such a system both elitist and something of a postcode lottery. What if two people presenting identical symptoms see the same assessor, but one has a different first language?

I appreciate this is idealistic given the nature of what we're dealing with, and of course I go through huge ups and downs like we all do. However, I've found it helpful to try to keep a positive mental attitude to life wherever possible. It might not help the symptoms but it can certainly make things feel that little bit more bearable. I never used to be like this. Experience had taught me situations typically didn't end well for me, and my inherent negativity was one thing my ex had a point about.

The catalyst for changing my outlook was a chance encounter I had with a gentleman back in 2016. I was over in Belfast, recording some music with my mate Frankie, and one night we went to a bar called The Ceili House in the nearby town of Coalisland, where he was performing a set. After he'd played, and after a lot of Guinness, we were sat outside and met a gaunt-looking man in a bowler hat who was having a smoke. As is the way in Ireland, we got chatting.

'I'm 48 and I've got leukaemia, lads,' he said. Frank and I looked at each other awkwardly. The chap's face lit up. 'But I don't give a fuck!' he beamed. 'I'm living my life to the full. I'm going out with a great big fucking smile on my face!' He stubbed his cigarette out and began to hobble back to the bar, before turning around and adding, 'And, hopefully, a giant boner!' He laughed and went on his way. In the most unoriginal of fashions, I remember thinking that if he could be that positive given his situation, there's no reason I couldn't at least make more of an effort myself.

Staying motivated despite our troubles is definitely tough, but it *can* be done with practice. Instead of focusing on how things used to be and how rubbish we're feeling now, the goal is to think more about all we're still able to do, despite the adversity. They probably won't be huge things, but any achievements are big for us under the circumstances. Another part of my therapy at the Maudsley was keeping a 'successes diary': a log of all the good things happening in my life that I was still managing to accomplish. It sounds a bit flowery, but I think it was useful. They weren't ever huge bombshells – more like 'guitar pedal manufacturer liked the demo video I shot for them' and 'made nice pizza – my best dough yet' – but actively giving more mental focus to those things rather than the DPD did help me to see that my current situation isn't *all* bad. Dr Hallett explains the theory behind the exercise:

> Imagine a magnet with both positive and negative poles. In clients with strongly held negative core beliefs, the negative pole is working much harder than the positive pole, so over time the individual gathers in mainly negative information about themselves and others, reinforcing their negative views. In therapy, we try to work at weakening this mental habit as it can cause entrenched mood problems and prevent individuals from reaching their goals. One of the ways this can be achieved is to strengthen the positive pole of the magnet (that is, deliberately build up a new evidence bank).

Yes, I'm living with my parents in my thirties – that doesn't make me feel good – but I have a roof over my head and no big financial worries (that aren't foolishly guitar-related, anyway), and that's something I need be thankful for. A lot of people aren't so lucky.

To this end, the managing of expectations was another revelation I took away from CBT. I would feel especially low whenever I'd travel abroad, as it was the time I most desperately wanted to be able to 'experience' new things, yet when I got off the plane my mood would dive as I was just as numb as back in England. What I was doing was setting myself up for a very obvious fail – *of course* I was going to feel removed from the situation. The DPD wasn't going to have miraculously vanished during a couple of hours on an EasyJet. Now, I try go away *accepting* that nothing is going to seem real. It's definitely become more difficult to justify spending money on 'experiences' rather than tangible objects, but having more realistic expectations about them has certainly helped.

Social activities are easy to let fall by the wayside without a concerted effort. I was never one for going out every night with my friends – far from it – but whenever I make arrangements, I always do my best to honour them. More often than not I *really* don't look forward to them. I always think I'll be too tired, would rather be in bed and we'll probably end up talking about how great my friends' lives are. But almost always, I feel glad I went once I get home. Social situations – even occasionally, for an introvert – can energize us. Isolation doesn't go hand-in-hand with good mental health, as many reports following Covid-19 lockdowns confirmed. Try not to predict a negative outcome for situations without evidence to back that thought up – that's what psychologists call *catastrophizing*. Staying in touch with people close to us is important.

This is probably a sensible point to discuss the changing ways

I've tackled the issue of my DPD with my friends. Back at university, I wish I'd had the knowledge to talk to Josh about what was going on and how much I was struggling but I just didn't have the means to verbalize it. It was important to me that he knew something was going on, so I would tell him I was going to one of my sessions, but that's all I really felt able to say.

As soon as I discovered the condition, I wanted to be more open but didn't know how to go about it. I settled on writing everything down in a letter and gradually sending it to a few of my closest friends. I think this was a good move as it didn't create any awkward face-to-face conversations. It allowed people to know what was going on and gave *them* the choice as to whether they wanted to discuss it further. It also let them consider it in their own time without feeling they needed to react in any particular way. To me, it was the most gentle and polite way of broaching the subject with people with whom I might not have had the relationship necessary to bring it up in casual conversation. Men especially have, in my experience, seemed notoriously bad at discussing our mental health with other men, and I very much considered myself part of that problem.

If you think writing something down is an approach that might work for you, or even if you're just curious about how I worded it to my friends, I've reproduced that letter at the end of this book. Please feel free to use it as a template to help you explain your struggles if it's appropriate to do so.

The reaction to sending it around was generally very positive. Even though it was a million miles away from the sort of thing I'd usually chat to my friends about, most picked up on the honesty of it and were very kind. My best friends were, without exception, absolutely lovely – saying things like 'Thank you for telling me/I'm here if you need to chat/Please let me know if I can help at all/etc.', which were all very comforting responses to receive after opening up about something so personal. Especially since getting the official diagnosis, everybody I've told has been brilliant. I really do have some fantastic mates.

However, this hasn't always been the case. It's painful to say it, but I've completely lost friends through opening up about my mental health. Generally, I've just received the silent treatment, but other times, things have been more to the point. One person told me very directly why they were choosing to never talk to me again. I can't remember their exact words, but the gist of it was 'I think you're a ticking timebomb and I'm not dealing with you when you go off'. We'd been friends for ten years.

Whenever this has happened, it's been easy to wheel out the old clichéd mantra of social bravado: 'Oh well, if they're going to be like that, they can't have been a good friend to begin with. Good riddance, I'm better off without them!' But let's be honest: it hurts. It always confuses me slightly when I think about those reactions afterwards, because I'm still the exact same person I was two minutes beforehand. They'd known for years I was having struggles and they were fine with that. But giving the struggles a name was enough to make them recoil and want nothing more to do with me – sometimes after being friends for most of our lives. As Mara explains:

> It might be an impression, but I felt like their approach towards me changed a bit afterwards. Same kindness, but more distance and less confidence.

I think the biggest trigger I've found when talking about DPD has been the word 'psychiatric' – it's usually at that point people begin to act weird. It's one of those words that can mean a huge breadth of things: from a 50mg antidepressant to Broadmoor.[2] I'm speculating here, and possibly unfairly, but I swear I've seen the cogs whirring inside people's brains and seen them decide I must be dangerous to be around. One ex-friend excused themselves from our drink date and hastily left the bar just a few minutes after I mentioned that word and their facial expression dropped. They've never replied to any of my messages since.

Sometimes, I've tried to rekindle things after a sensible amount of time, generally through a WhatsApp message on their birthday asking how they are. Usually it's been ignored, and occasionally my number was already blocked. Whenever I *have* heard back, I've been haunted by an old familiar phrase: 'Hope you're well.' A rough translation is: 'I'm going to give the illusion of being friendly but I don't wish to receive a reply or engage with you any further.'

In a similar vein, I've really had come to terms with the pressures that are put on us in society. From a young age, we get the 'typical' path drummed into us – or at least, it was for me growing up in the 90s. You go to school, get qualifications, find a job, meet somebody, buy a house, get married, have kids, etc. Of course, nowadays it's accepted that many of those things are either unnecessary or idealistic (does any young person own their home anymore?), but even so, I think the social pressures are still there.

That's all they are, though: social pressures. They're not rules. I've really felt bad over the years about my life situation, but that's largely because society has told me I should. To say that 'everybody is on a different path' sounds like a weak line from a motivational speech but it really is true – just because one person marries and

---

2   A high-security psychiatric hospital in Berkshire, England. It's a bit of a 'buzz word' in the British press for the more extreme end of the psychiatric illness spectrum.

another never does doesn't mean the latter is a 'failure', for example. Yet, many (usually older) people would shake their head and say, 'Oh, they never married. Such a shame for them.' We find ourselves in this unique environment nowadays where different generations struggle more than ever to comprehend another's point of view because so much has changed in such a short timeframe. I tend to think of Baby Boomers as being products of the stoic 'Keep Calm and Carry On' generation – literally 'Suppress emotions, keep face. And if you don't talk about your problems, they're not real.'

Stigma surrounding mental health and invisible illnesses absolutely still exists. I think it's getting better but it's far from uncommon to encounter hostility when opening up about a mental health condition, especially online. As I said earlier, people have a tougher time believing the things they can't reaffirm with their own eyes; so, when an illness might not be obvious, it can be a battle to get people on your side.

A tradesman fitting some windows here once introduced himself with, 'Urgh... You're so spoilt, aren't you? Here at your age on your 'life-long gap year'... Yeah, I'm onto you!' My mother was once sarcastically asked, 'And how's Joe then? Last I heard he was still squatting at home and not doing anything with his life?' One Sunday morning I woke up to about 15 emails sat in my inbox – at 2am, somebody had signed me up to a load of job-search websites using the keyword 'McDonald's'. I certainly have the utmost respect for anybody who works hard in this world to support themselves but I'm assuming this wasn't intended to be flattering.

These are by no means particularly brutal examples, but they still hurt. They're all times where people have judged my situation without actually understanding anything about it. This has been a hard lesson to learn: everybody loves to have opinions about things they don't understand. You'll never stop that – and we all do it, if we're honest. You just have to try your hardest not to let it shake you up when you're feeling bad and somebody decides to voice one.

Opening up online can be particularly fraught, because your thoughts appear in front of people who can then respond anonymously and with few or no consequences to their actions. It feels like comments sections are often viewed as a licence to say whatever you want, regardless of how offensive it might be. Through her YouTube channel, dodie has been raising awareness of DPD by being open about her struggles:

> Mostly the response is really kind – way more than I was expecting, and way more [kind] than I would have been when I was younger. There is so much bad that comes with it though. When I was getting the rTMS [Repetitive Transcranial Magnetic Stimulation] treatment, BBC 5 Live wanted to do an interview while I was getting it done … They put it up on their Facebook page, which is full of Boomers, and all of them were just like, 'What's this crazy Millennial doing?! Just go help your mom with the dishes!' But then there were some people who said they'd felt like this for years and didn't know what it was, so, it was still so worth it.

I've come to realize just how many emotional abusers there are in this world – people who thrive on treating others badly and 'manage' their own problems by lashing out unnecessarily. A common tactic of these sorts of people is gaslighting – saying something nasty and inflammatory, then when offence is taken, making the victim doubt themselves and feel *they're* in the wrong because of how *they've chosen* to react to the remark. It's where a lot of internet 'trolling' stems from

– people dishing out unsolicited personal attacks, then branding their victims as 'Generation Snowflake' if they dare to defend themselves.

These sorts of people are everywhere, and mental health is an area they love to prey on. I've been called a 'nutter' and a 'psycho'. I've been told to 'fuck off back to the looney bin' and then berated with the likes of 'Don't throw your toys out of the pram. It's not me who has the "issues"' when I've stood my ground. It's emotionally manipulative and it's absolutely not your fault if you encounter assholes like this. Sadly, it's 'sport' for them, and the more you rise to it and show you're angry, the more powerful they feel. They want to know they've gotten under your skin. That response is their reward.

There's a real power and satisfaction to just walking away from these people and not rising to the bait. Without your reaction, they have nothing but their own misery. That's how I deal with the unsubstantiated nastiness that gets thrown my way online. As silent magician Teller once said about performing to rowdy audiences: 'You feel like an idiot if you're heckling a silent guy' (2017). Absolutely stand up for yourself – I'm not saying you should submissively accept abuse. But sometimes, understanding that a bully wants your reaction is the best way to strip them of their power.

More than any of the CBT-derived 'life hacks' that have reduced my rumination and helped me structure my life in a more productive and healthy way, understanding this psychology of other people and challenging the reasons why I was feeling my life was an abject failure have easily been my most important takeaways from therapies. Granted, my DPD symptoms haven't improved. But this knowledge has changed my life so much for the better and made it easier to cope with the way things are for me nowadays. Trauma therapies really opened my eyes to the fact that a lot of things I spent years beating myself up over simply weren't my fault.

We're encouraged to think within the same societal tramlines when it comes to defining our 'success': qualifications, bank balance, the number of cars on the driveway, the size of a house, how big our television is, the 'status' of the job we work, etc. They're all very measurable things stemming from a capitalist society. Plus, they're what bullies typically latch onto to quickly drill for the nerve – we're so conditioned to put emphasis on them that we tend to be very touchy whenever they're called into question. It's what the kids at school did: they took any insecurity they knew I had (there were many) and tightened the screw, because reinforcing my own negative self-beliefs was easier than making new ones.

I can't overstress how much redefining what 'success' is has helped me in my daily battles of living with DPD. The standard societal measures are rubbish – and, I think, dangerous. I don't earn much money, I can't support myself, I still live with my parents, my car is old, I don't have many friends and I've never done much good in the world. Until the last few years that's made me feel like I've completely screwed *everything* up – despite knowing that the underlying reason for lots of those things has been my illness. So, am I a total failure?

No. Getting up in the morning when it feels like nothing is real is a success. Receiving kind words from somebody saying you've helped them with a problem is a success. Setting yourself a small goal and achieving it despite the adversities in your way is a success. Beating an addiction is a success. Making a new friend is a success. And, when you're routinely feeling like you want to give up on life, just keeping going is the biggest fucking success you can possibly have.

9.
I Love You (in Principle)

DPD and Relationships

Relationships are difficult enough to maintain in the best of circumstances. Taking two individuals' wants, needs and interests, slamming them together in a way that both are satisfied with, and keeping the whole machine functioning well enough to have longevity is a complex tapestry of compromise, communication and strong emotions. But when one person is living with a chronic illness, it's always going to throw things out of balance.

Since starting my YouTube channel *DPD Diaries*, I've been surprised by the number of partners who have written to me asking for advice on their relationships – far more so than sufferers themselves – and my videos on this topic have been some of the most watched on the channel. I think this is a positive sign overall but, under the surface, it's a strong indication that being in a relationship with a DPD sufferer is far from plain sailing. The condition places a lot of storms in the paths of couples and makes their journeys more treacherous.

I also want to give my partner, Sophie, a voice in this chapter, as she's been on the frontline dealing with me – both as a boyfriend and a DPD sufferer. You know how hard things are for me, but I think it's also important to hear how my struggles have directly impacted somebody else. She's never been one to hold back on hard truths either, so I dare say I might get a kicking.

I've never been one for casual dating, so my experiences are only really based on a few longer-term relationships. But struggles with my head thing have absolutely been a factor in the downfall of my past ones – from both sides of the equation. I was as open as I could possibly be about what I was going through and described the symptoms using all the metaphors I could muster. I've always been totally honest when it's come to opening up to romantic partners. But once the honeymoon periods expired, I quickly learned that knowing about a problem and working to accommodate it are two things that don't necessarily come together.

Being in a relationship with DPD involved is *not* easy. It's going to make everything hard; there's no avoiding that. Things can be incredibly frustrating. There will probably be times you both question if it's possible to continue. But maintaining the relationship is absolutely doable provided both parties are willing to work at it and as long as you both want things to work out. When someone isn't truly committed, things will boil over and burn you very quickly. It takes a lot of effort. No war was ever won by leaving things to chance.

I always say it takes a very particular type of person to be in a relationship with a DPD sufferer, largely because of the condition's invisible nature. There needs to be a huge amount of trust between two people when one is describing something it's impossible for the other to see and asking them to accept it 100 per cent as being 'just the way things are'. Moreover, if the sufferer has emotional numbing, that adds a whole further tier of complexity. Choosing to be in a relationship with somebody who feels they have to say '*I'm not able to feel love for you*' requires a level of understanding and compassion so deep that it can be tough to comprehend. It can be even more difficult if a person develops DPD *during* a relationship as that will require an abrupt readjustment for both parties. I put off getting into another relationship for years after my previous one because of how badly the head thing impacted it. But eventually I decided it was worth the risk to commit to Sophie. Here are her words:

> The 'can't feel love' thing catches people off-guard. One or two have asked how I deal with it. It's fairly easy: I trust Joe's judgement of what his brain is trying to tell him. He's also a much kinder individual than he gives himself credit for. Just because it's numbed, doesn't mean the emotion isn't in there somewhere. The scariest thing he's said to me is that sometimes he has to remind himself who I am when he first sees me in the morning. That's nothing I've taken personal offence to – it's more a terror in what this disorder has done to his brain, how it's clouded so much. He has to remind himself continually what is real and what is a dream. As far as he's concerned, I might be a hallucination.

Accepting there's a problem in the first place might sound like a blindingly obvious thing to say, but I think it can often be overlooked. It's impossible to move forward with a DPD-centric relationship without both people knowing exactly where they stand and having an open dialogue about how they're both feeling. Dynamics will deteriorate if crucial issues are ignored and frustrations are left to fester. There needs to be a constant two-way flow of honesty and communication. The sufferer needs to explain to their partner how things are for them, how they might be struggling with a certain situation or commitment and how their partner can help to support them. The partner needs to trust that their sufferer is telling the truth, accept that sometimes they might not be able to fulfil commitments and not make them feel bad about any shortcomings that might result. It can be very tough to know that somebody you care about is going through such deep and disturbing issues, but responding with kindness and support is so important, especially when they're having a particularly hellish time. That's not to say a laugh can't be handy on occasion – Sophie and I both acknowledge my emotional numbing with jokey comments like 'I love you...in principle!' and 'What do you feel about that? Well, aside from nothing!' As long as you share a sense of humour and you're on the same page with what's appropriate, I don't think it's bad to find the funnies *sometimes*.

In the past though, I've fallen flat on my face trying to manage this. I was always very conflict-shy in relationships and found it much easier to make jokes about things that were bothering me than tackle the issue head-on. If I felt the person was treating me unfairly over the head thing, for example, I'd default to laughing about it as a way to bring it up in conversation, but that also gave me an easy, 'I was only joking!' get-out clause if things became heated. It was purely a coping mechanism rather than any sort of resolution. I didn't want the agro as it'd make me feel even more stressed than the matter itself. It was *such* an unhealthy approach though, as it never resolved anything – and worse than that, it meant small issues grew into much bigger ones because they were never nipped in the bud. Sophie and I are both very good at letting each other know in a respectful way if we have a problem – and through doing that, even with complex and trying DPD matters, we're usually able to understand each other simply by talking it through.

Something Joe has always been very wary of is having his disorder held against him when he has already explained how it can affect him - such as being distant or struggling if he spends too long in certain situations. Occasionally it amazes me how long he can endure through things with how he's feeling. Patience is important and you need to learn when your partner looks like they're starting to flag. Joe goes quiet, his eyes glaze and sometimes go a bit red, his head will bow and sometimes I'll notice his fists clench - not in anger but to distract himself from what else is going on. If you're someone more likely to have a go at your partner for 'being embarrassing' at a social event due to an illness, this isn't the relationship for you. If either of you are expecting the other to read minds, it isn't going to work. You really do need to be able to talk about everything.

Really knowing your partner and having their back is a key skill that both parties need to develop:

Jenny adds:

My boyfriend has started being good at noticing when I've not been mentally present. I'll have trouble talking and be a passive observer of life. I'm sort of okay, except that I can't really interact that much.

Sometimes I'm quite happy to go on a day trip, but other times I know I need to stay close to home in case I start to crumble. Similarly, Sophie and I will often sit and chat for hours, but if I'm having an especially tough time, we both know conversation kills me and we're quite comfortable sitting in silence. The only time I find myself getting frustrated with her is when she tries to push me to do something

I'm not feeling up to. Her suggestions are always in my best interests, but if I'm exhausted or feeling especially low, I don't want to go for a long walk or cook a nice dinner. Being honest about your state of mind at any given time is important to avoid 'situations'.

When partners ask me for advice, I always encourage them, before anything else, to gather a basic understanding of what the condition is and how it can affect people. In the same way that knowing the psychology behind DPD can help a sufferer take away some of the fear, partners typically find it easier to accept their loved one acting a certain way if they understand *why*. You don't have to become a psychiatrist, but checking a few websites or videos is a helpful starting point. Asking questions is good too, as the condition affects everybody differently (e.g. 'I read DPD makes some people physically numb. Do you get that?'). Showing an interest and making an effort to comprehend what they're going through will mean the world to the sufferer – trust me.

Somebody who has done just that is Katherine. Her boyfriend Peter has DPD, and early on in their relationship she struggled with feeling like he was giving her mixed signals. Of course, it was the effects of his condition – he thought she might not want to be with him if she knew about it. They slowly began to talk it through and have since worked together over many years to learn to support each other. Katherine recently enrolled on a course in Denmark for partners of people with mental health problems to learn how to better support Peter. She says:

> I have also experienced some mental difficulties, and still do. But I think that I easily fall into the role of a 'helper', maybe to bring focus away from my own issues. But I was tired of the role and I felt it created distance between us when I tried to help too much ... I am already learning a lot on the course. People who have partners

> with mental illnesses often try to control things – but we cannot. We cannot control if our partner is confused or is suffering. I do not think about when and how the DPD will go away anymore. I guess that I have accepted that it is a part of him at the moment. But it does not define him. Of course, there are still things that are difficult, but I really want to be with him. He is one of the most creative, sensitive and funny people I know.

As Katherine's also found though, it's important to acknowledge that unless they've been through it themselves, a partner won't ever *truly* understand how a sufferer experiences the world. Theory can only get you so far in terms of really *getting* the condition. We struggle to communicate and explain our symptoms to everybody, which of course includes partners. There's a lot to be said for gaining a knowledge of what DPD is, but it needs to be accepted there'll always be an upper limit in terms of being able to relate to the condition, especially in a *life* sense: how absolutely helpless and empty it can make somebody feel despite them outwardly seeming 'normal' is nigh on impossible to grasp.

This is very true for the bigger picture. DPD limits our abilities to be flexible and accommodate somebody else's needs on top of looking after ourselves – and that can make big life decisions even more difficult. Jen says:

> It's hard for a partner to accept that their life is going to be different and travel that new journey with you. They have to make a choice.

I've heard from parents who have told me they're unable to feel any love for their newborn child but are scared to try explaining that to their partner, which is logical but heartbreaking at the same time.

When you're struggling so much that you have to be supported in your living, and any sense of vague familiarity you can cling onto feels like a lifeline, it can cause problems. This is something I've found very difficult.

A good example of this happened recently. In 2019, Sophie moved 200 miles away to study for a master's degree. This was tough in some ways, but the fact that it was only for nine months made it alright. But she was then offered the chance to study for a PhD, which would have involved her moving away more permanently. This presented something of a dilemma for us as a couple. Through lack of funds primarily, but a need for stability and my loud recording equipment also, I wouldn't have been able to move with her. We both knew that. Equally, I didn't want her to turn down the opportunity because of me, as it would have made me feel like I'd shackled her down and my DPD was now holding somebody else back in life as well as myself. She's always said she has to include me as a factor in her decisions, which I do understand, but it makes me feel horrendous that I can have a negative effect on her life because of how inflexible I have to be. She decided – for several reasons – not to go for it in the end, but knowing I played a part in that doesn't make me feel good. Sophie says:

> 'What are your plans?' becomes a stressful question to answer from friends. Joe is very cautious about how all this affects me and insists he shouldn't be a factor in my own life-planning. But it's impossible to not think about your partner at all. I turned down what lots of people would see as a golden opportunity – Joe couldn't just up sticks and move with me. It mostly wasn't down to Joe that much in the end, although being that far away made the opportunity less appealing. Maybe I would have been more of a risk-taker if I wasn't with Joe? Maybe being with Joe is a risk

in itself? I don't like to think about it like that though. One of the most difficult things for me isn't the disorder itself; it's trying to explain it to other people. Because Joe can appear 'normal' and saves up his energy for these instances, it can be hard for others to understand that he has a 24/7 problem.

If somebody in your life has any form of mental health problem – especially one that others won't have heard of – it's a good idea to give some thought to how you might explain it when people inevitably ask. In the same way that I've had to arm myself with analogies and rehearse my response to 'So, what do you do?', this is something that affects the people who know me too – not just Sophie but parents and friends. Having a pre-prepared answer to offer people when they ask about your loved one – and maybe misunderstand their situation – can be important for avoiding confusion and staving off some of the more hurtful comments people throw around. If you're somebody with lived experience of the condition, being able to enlighten others with facts and appropriate descriptions is a vital skill. Offering to accompany a sufferer to their medical appointments can be another valuable way to show support. We aren't always good at being put on the spot or remembering things that are said, so having somebody who's informed with us to help fill in key details and remember what the clinician said can be a huge deal.

The 'overspill' effect of DPD does mean that its effect on relationships isn't limited to romantic ones. It affects our friendships and dynamics with relatives also. Often when we're feeling at our absolute worst, we have to rely on those closest to us for support. Jane goes through especially bad patches with her DPD and on occasion has had to leave her flat in London to stay with her mother on the south coast. Mary has first-hand experience of fulfilling the roles of both parent and carer when Jane has felt at her worst:

At those times, it's about being a constant positive and calm presence. Being there for her through every minute of every day – to the extent that I would sometimes sleep in the same room when she was at her most vulnerable, and encourage her to eat a little and take her medications. But the most important thing was trying to stabilize her mood and manage expectations. When she says, 'I can't do this again – I'm not strong enough,' I'll remind her of how strong she is and the small improvements she has already made. When she says, 'I'm never going to get better, am I?', I'll encourage her to think back to other times when she has and how much more we know now about how to manage it. It's not perfect of course. There are lots of tears and despair. And it is exhausting. We are fortunate that Jane is a positive person by nature and feels she has much to live for. She wants my support and is grateful for it. And, she trusts me.

For a parent, seeing your child struggling with a debilitating condition is one of the worst possible things to endure. Mary tells me of how heartbroken and frightened she's felt when not knowing how to best support Jane, the sense of inadequacy when she can't answer her big questions and the fear around what might happen when she's no longer around to care for Jane. DPD has an absolutely colossal impact on all the different relationships in our lives and affects everybody we're close to in different ways. But at the same time, Mary also tells me of how in awe she is of Jane's strength and grit despite her adversities:

I am so proud of the effort Jane puts into each and every day. I feel humbled by her tenacity and her positivity. And I feel inspired by her campaigning and by the work she has put into setting up the Unreal charity. She does have success in her life – a personal relationship, a home, a rewarding and demanding job – but she has always said to me that the most important work she does is to campaign on behalf of others who experience DPD, so that their experience in seeking understanding and support can be better than hers. Ultimately it is that which drives her.

None of it is easy – for anyone. Maintaining relationships, however, is so fundamentally important to our wellbeing. It can be done but it's something that takes a lot of perseverance and understanding from both sides. As with so many elements of our lives when an illness is involved, it's important to stress that relationships can still be incredibly fruitful and close, but they might just be a little different to how most others experience them. Yes, some people will not understand what we're going through – that's unfortunately inevitable. Many have found family members refusing to accept the problems they cannot see or are reluctant to even acknowledge. Looking after somebody with any illness can feel frustrating, and sometimes partners might misinterpret the things we try to say. But that absolutely doesn't mean that relationships are a no-go – there can be a huge depth and strength to them that both parties find incredibly enriching. Mental illnesses don't have to deny certain areas of life to us – in fact, I would say in some circumstances they can make our bonds stronger by giving us a deeper and more intimate understanding of others. As Sophie remarked when I ran this chapter past her:

I know you're suffering, but a lot of the time it's absolutely fine with you. It really is.

10.
Treating DPD

To cut to the chase and briefly answer the question everybody wants to know before we dive into discussing treatments in detail – I ask Dr Hunter whether it's possible to recover from long-term DPD. 'Yes – and completely recover,' she replies. Let's start as we mean to go on.

A hard reality before we do, though. I get emails and messages all the time asking about the 'cure' for DPD. Things like 'I've heard sublingual vitamin B12 cures this. Is that true?' and 'I need to be prescribed lamotrigine because I know that will cure me.' The honest truth of the matter is, there is no 'cure' – and by that, I mean there is no one single thing that works for everybody and guarantees symptoms disappear. There is no universal 'quick fix' or 'magic pill'. *Recovery* is possible but it's a personal journey involving an individualized approach based on your own set of circumstances – and often a fair bit of trial and error too. Somebody once said to me about the Maudsley, 'That place is like Area 51 – they don't want the secret to get out!' That isn't true at all – because there is no secret.

Some people – generally those with transient depersonalization – find their symptoms disappear fairly quickly on their own. But for others, especially those of us with long-term DPD, it can be much harder to treat and sometimes never goes away entirely. I don't want to begin this chapter on a downer, but expectations around recovery do need to be realistic. I've tried everything I possibly can for over a decade – countless courses of therapy, trialling medications, all the CBT strategies – and my symptoms are still getting worse over time. Treating DPD can quite often be a case of *easing* symptoms and learning to manage them, rather than pursuing a 'complete' disappearance. Dr Hunter explains:

> It's quite difficult to determine who will and who won't [recover]. I'm always very up-front with people, and I try not to have 'getting rid of it' as a goal ... It's more about understanding what is potentially keeping it going, looking at strategies for that, and looking back at why it got triggered in the first place.

Clinicians specializing in the condition are few and far between. In the UK there's the well-known Depersonalisation Disorder Service within the Maudsley Hospital in London, an NHS clinic only accessible by UK residents aged over 18. Dr Hunter – formerly the clinical lead there – now runs The Depersonalisation Clinic (thedepersonalisationclinic.com) where she offers self-funded and NHS-funded appointments both in-person and via video-conferencing, and sees adult patients as well as 16–18-year-olds (for whom until recently there was no provision) and clients based internationally. There's a handful of resources in the USA: the Mayo clinics advertise depersonalization-specific assessments and psychological therapies; and Dr Daphne Simeon (New York), Dr Elena Bezzubova (California) and Dr Orna Guralnik (New York) all have depersonalization expertise and offer private treatment. Finding an expert elsewhere in the world is a bit of a lottery – there are some resources out there (e.g. a depersonalization clinic within the Johannes Gutenberg University of Mainz in Germany), but it can take a lot of digging around to uncover them.

Getting to see a specialist can mean a lot of travelling. My weekly sessions at the Maudsley involved a three-hour bus journey each way – so although the sessions were only an hour, I was up at 6am and didn't get home until the evening, which would knock me out for a good couple of days afterwards. Those trips soon mounted up in terms of cost too. I came across somebody last year who had been approved for funded sessions at the Maudsley but had to resort to public crowdfunding to raise their travel money to get there. However, most therapists and organizations have moved their work online during the Covid-19 pandemic and it's likely many will continue this as an option into the future, even if it's not currently advertised – so it's worth an email if you'd like to see one of the above-mentioned specialists but don't live nearby. An online assessment (at least) by the likes of Dr Hunter can be invaluable, as the resulting report is a very authoritative document to present to a local psychologist or psychiatrist.

If you're unable to see somebody specializing in the condition specifically, Dr Guralnik offers some pointers as to what sort of therapist would be suitable.

> I'd recommend somebody with some kind of analytic training – meaning that they do deeper work and they can tolerate intensity... There's a school of psychoanalysis that is relational and those tend to be people who are more adept at focusing on the here and now, the immediacy, the spontaneous and authentic things that unfold between them and their patients. Those are

typically the therapists that would do better work with people
with depersonalization.

I'd add that therapists with a background in trauma are a good option
too – mainly because dissociative symptoms are so common in that
field. They might not have come across DPD specifically, but they're
more likely to be familiar with the sensations you're describing. You
do need to build up a working relationship with your therapist, so
they'll ultimately need to be somebody you can get on with and
connect with also.

A difficulty with treating DPD – and most mental health conditions, I suppose – is accurately monitoring and measuring the
symptoms. As well as being more visible, physical health problems
are often easier to treat. If you break your ankle, you tell your doctor
it's agony when you walk, they take an X-ray, see the fracture, put it
in plaster for eight weeks and you both know it's better when you
can go for a jog. It's a fairly clear-cut process.

However, when a problem affects us psychologically, treating it
is more of an abstract process open to individual interpretation –
generally based on what we're able to verbalize as a patient. This is
yet another reason the chronic lack of awareness about DPD is such
a problem: clinicians aren't aware of it existing and therefore commonly misdiagnose it – even though when we sufferers come across
a list of symptoms, they're painfully specific and unquestionably
accurate for us.

Mental health services are quite reliant on stats and figures to
measure problems and gauge the effectiveness of treatment. As
soon as you become involved in any area of a service dealing with
psychological difficulties, you'll almost certainly come across questionnaires that put a numerical figure on your symptoms. These are

useful as they can highlight subtle changes in the patient that they might not be aware of, especially when going through therapies that discourage the constant monitoring of sensations. The *DSM-5* (APA 2013) and *ICD-10-CM* (AMA 2020) diagnostic tools are commonly used in services all around the world to diagnose mental health problems – and the questionnaires are generally derived from their criteria. For me, in UK primary care services, these have usually been the PHQ-9 and GAD-7 forms, which are based on the *DSM* criteria for depression and anxiety.

A more reliable psychometric test for us is the Cambridge Depersonalization Scale – 29 questions grading symptoms of depersonalization specifically on a scale of 0 to 10, with a score of over 70 indicating DPD. It's likely that if you're in therapy specifically for DPD you'll be asked to fill this questionnaire in at regular intervals. However, it's freely available online, so you can do it yourself if you want to monitor your symptoms, and the results can be another useful thing to present to a doctor. For what it's worth, the last time I took this test I scored 224 – so the DPD diagnosis is fairly robust.

A comment that gets thrown my way fairly often online about DPD recovery is 'It just goes away', which, of course, has not been the case for me. Transient depersonalization by its nature comes and goes, which is where I think most of these comments stem from – as Professor David points out:

> Given that a lot of people will say they have had depersonalization symptoms (at least in questionnaires or telephone surveys) but don't have DPD, it must get better on its own in the vast majority.

This makes sense: transient depersonalization has to get better to be defined as 'transient' (and not a disorder) in the first place.

However, I've heard of people who have had chronic DPD for many years and have then recovered without professional help. I ask Dr Hunter whether it's possible to recover from long-term DPD without professional intervention: She replies:

> Absolutely - there are people who 'naturally' recover. In a way, what we are trying to do in therapy is enhance that, but also see where people have got stuck.

This happened to Jane when her first bout of DPD abated following a period of using her own distraction techniques. She has since relapsed, but the memory of recovering is a vibrant one.

> I started to have moments where I could sit and be aware that my consciousness was working smoothly - I could just sit with it for a bit of time ... Eventually, I started to have the ability to sit on my own in a room, bring my mind to focus on whether I was well and present or experiencing that 'clunky' consciousness, and travel around my head, being aware that I was completely present in the world. Before that time, I was running around doing a lot of distracting myself. But that time when I could just sit and realize that I was living again, and was present again, gave me the most enormous sense of peace. I think I did less that year than I'd done in the previous years with the depersonalization - because it wasn't about achieving, or distracting ... I could just sit and 'be' ... that was enough.

I do think the 'It just goes away' comments highlight a stumbling block for the wider public discussion around DPD recovery. In the same way that the condition affects us all differently and we all have different underlying factors keeping it going, the same is absolutely true for recovery. I genuinely think I 'simply' haven't yet identified and addressed my underlying problem(s) – one day I will, and I will recover. I have to believe that for my own sanity. People who have encountered brief transient depersonalization can be quick to assume their experience and route out of it must be the same as for somebody who has suffered with it solidly for years. One person commented underneath my short film saying, 'You need to stop being a self-pitying little bitch', and another explained how their son had battled DPD for eight years before writing a farewell letter and ending his own life. If anything highlights a failing to understand the differing extremes, it's seeing those two comments sitting side by side in the public domain. People who flippantly tell me that I 'just need to laugh at my depersonalization and it'll go, no problem' haven't quite grasped what it's like to have decades of your life destroyed by a chronic illness that endless professional interventions haven't been able to touch. I love hearing people's recovery stories – I honestly do – but it needs to be understood that one individual's success doesn't mean they've then unlocked the secret for everybody else.

When professional treatment does become necessary, a key factor in its effectiveness is an early intervention – Professor David notes:

> It is a truism of medicine that the longer a condition goes on, the harder it is to shift.

This is yet another problem of the high diagnosis period: if the thought processes and self-beliefs that are keeping the DPD going are allowed to develop unchallenged for all those years, and the additional distress of experiencing the symptoms can exacerbate the cycle, the condition is likely to be far more deep-rooted by the time actual treatment begins. I can only imagine how differently things might have played out for me if when I first approached the doctor they'd said, 'Sounds like anxiety – it'll pass. *But*, if it doesn't, it might be depersonalization disorder, and we can refer you for specialist psychological therapy.'

Early on in your journey, clinicians will want to rule out the potential for other things to be causing the symptoms. Dr Guralnik explains:

> Once you know a person is experiencing depersonalization and not something else, it's very important to do a differential diagnosis to make sure there isn't some other process going on that is primary ... whether it's the beginning of a psychotic process, or some kind of bipolar shift, or a severe depression where someone can be so flattened out mood-wise that they can feel depersonalized because the bottom of their emotional floor has dropped out. Then it's not really primary depersonalization; it's secondary to something else.

This is one of the early steps to figuring out what might ultimately be driving your symptoms – it'll help everybody figure out the best way to help you going forwards.

The primary treatment for DPD is psychological therapy, which can take many different forms depending on your case. The type of therapies given need to match up with the specific reason(s) your DPD is believed to be perpetuating – there isn't one single structure that can apply to everybody. But that said, most therapy for DPD does involve at least some CBT techniques: examining your daily life, changing your routines and thinking patterns, and challenging your self-beliefs. For example, the 'successes diary' I kept at the

Maudsley was to encourage me not to focus on what I've lost but to put the spotlight on things that could be celebrated instead. We also identified the fact that my social interactions are quite limited – and although that's not necessarily out of keeping for an introvert and can have a positive effect on somebody with limited finances, humans are fundamentally social beings. Building more connections with others has been a focal point for me in recent years.

Although the therapy does ultimately need to be individualized, there is a general structure that Dr Hunter will typically begin with when starting work with a new patient. She explains:

> There is a framework. For example, we'll often start with a 'Five Ps' CBT model – which stands for Predisposing (things that might have been going on in the background), Precipitating (all the stuff that happens on the precipice before you fall off the edge), Presenting (usually depersonalization, but this can also be anxiety, depression, low self-esteem, etc.), Perpetuating (the things that are keeping it going) and Protective factors (things that might be working to your advantage). We can then look at making changes to those things we've identified: challenging thoughts, changing the processes, etc. We're looking at each of those factors and seeing what we can do to break the vicious cycles. So, there is some structure; a sort-of template.
>
> ... For people who have had it longer term – who are often still quite young but had it for years – they'll still likely have a lot of those predisposing factors still at play. We have to keep drilling into what's keeping this going; or if it's become a habit, how we can find a new way of 'being'.

As noted earlier, many of the 'life hacks' discussed in the previous chapter came about as a direct result of CBT – and with a lot of DPD treatment focusing on managing symptoms and helping us to function more productively despite them (rather than 'getting rid' of them), those techniques have absolutely been part of my treatment rather than being 'just' interim coping strategies. The key objectives of most of those techniques is reducing the constant monitoring of symptoms and our repeated questioning of reality. Dr Černis explains:

> Sometimes when you look at a word for too long, it starts to not look real. I think people accidentally do this to themselves with their thoughts and their body - the more you focus on it, the more you think, 'Is this real? Is this strange?'

This is similar to how Dr Ciaunica describes obsessively focusing on our disrupted sense of self:

> You are tempted to think even more about it because you see something is wrong. You see there is a crack on the window, and you are so obsessed by the crack that you keep looking ... but the more you look, the more it cracks!

Scrutinizing what we're feeling – or not feeling – can exacerbate the unreality by then feeding back into itself.

Treating transient depersonalization and DPD are similar in their approaches, but, typically, any depersonalization that fluctuates in intensity is easier to work with as it's more easily manipulated. The ups and downs can be measured with CBT tools such as 'intensity diaries' (grading the strength of the depersonalization on an hourly basis over a few weeks) and then, with your therapist, steps can be taken to identify patterns and reduce stressors to flatten the peaks.

Dr Hunter told me about a recent patient of hers who made enough progress to warrant discharge after just *three* sessions, although she stresses that was unusual. When you understand what is ultimately causing or exacerbating the depersonalization, you have much more power to fight it. Even for those who have chronic DPD but find the intensity of their symptoms varies, this can give therapists clues as to what might ultimately be driving it. Changes don't happen for no reason – exploring them can suggest how to manipulate things to your advantage.

Sometimes with DPD, though, the peaks and troughs aren't really there, and this is where depersonalization has become a sort of 'mode' rather than anything that moves around. This is where I find myself: my symptoms never really get better or worse but they do drop periodically – why it happens in this way, nobody seems to know. In instances such as mine, the underlying factors can be much trickier to identify and involve a lot of digging on the part of the therapist. Dr Hunter elaborates:

> I think it's important to see depersonalization – both transient and chronic – as a response to another problem. So, if you can work out what the underlying issue is, you should get the depersonalization to alleviate. But with some people it's become more entrenched and you have to do some more advanced techniques to get that to shift ... I quite like some of the tools from Schema therapy for when depersonalization has become a sort-of long-term coping mechanism. Within that, you can help people to see that the healthy 'adult' way of feeling emotions and dealing with them has been overwhelmed. That's where therapy needs to be more individualized – for a therapist, it helps to be able to bring an outsider's perspective on what might be driving it.

Challenging negative personality traits and self-beliefs is often a key area of therapy – as the emotional difficulties many DPD sufferers faced during childhood create issues that haunt us in adulthood. Even if the traits themselves aren't negative as such, sessions can involve looking at the pros and cons of 'being' a certain way and adapting your behaviours to compromise if, on balance, they might be doing you more harm than good. A lot of my CBT has centred around my tendencies towards *perfectionism*, which in some ways is positive: it means things get done on time and things get done well. I either do something to the absolute best of my abilities or I don't bother doing it at all. I've always felt this has given me some sense of integrity. In my mind, I'm more likely to be successful with things if I use a sledgehammer to crack a nut, so to speak.

However, it also means I lie awake analysing how to make things better. It causes stress levels to remain elevated. It's likely rooted in people pleasing, a leftover from my desperation to be accepted at school. If I do something and fail – or even if I simply don't achieve my own high expectations for myself – the comedown hits me even harder as I gave it everything and still didn't make the mark. That makes me feel I'm rubbish, reinforces the belief that my life really hasn't gone to plan, and I struggle to deal with it. I believe I look like an amateur.

So, you can see how it goes either way – CBT therapists might refer to that as *all-or-nothing thinking*: only seeing the extremes of a scenario. It's been identified that this could be feeding into my DPD, keeping stress levels high and my standards for myself even higher as I worry about tiny details nobody else will even notice. Then when I don't do something perfectly (because humans never do), I feel I've completely failed, even though it might have been successful on balance. A lot of my therapy has focused around accepting the middle ground and making more balanced appraisals, rather than defaulting to 'I screwed up' simply because one person might not like something I've done.

If your DPD has roots in traumatic events in your past, specific trauma therapies are often used. I've had a couple of these in the past, Eye Movement Desensitization and Reprogramming (EMDR) being the main one. Going through it was a weird experience: talking through difficult memories whilst looking at a bar of flashing lights, holding vibrating pads in my hands and listening to beeps through a set of headphones. It's also done by therapists asking the patient to watch their hand waving slowly back and forth, which is the original and more traditional method. The theory goes that you're better able to process a traumatic memory when your senses are partially diverted, as it can prevent extreme emotional reactions disrupting the flow of the work (Healthline 2019). Remember, the amygdala is a sensory part of the brain, and by distracting your senses you can fool its alarm mechanism somewhat and better access unresolved trauma without it kicking off. As one sufferer told me:

> Talking about DPD means confronting trauma my mind isn't ready to face, so when I try to talk, my mind dissociates to avoid bringing it up.

For this reason, EMDR is a common treatment for PTSD, especially if you suffer with flashbacks.

The psychological therapies listed here are by no means the only ones used for DPD – they're just some of the most common. Schema therapy, for example, is favoured by Dr Hunter for addressing some of the more ingrained negative self-beliefs and examining the ways in which we process emotions. Jen has found relief from Compassion Focused Therapy (CFT):

> I have high expectations of myself and feel huge disappointment when I don't get things right. My therapist taught me about self-compassion. I remember thinking, 'Wow, maybe we are not meant to beat ourselves up all the time!'

A sufferer in South Africa has been trying Acceptance and Commitment Therapy (ACT):

> It involves facing things that cause you anxiety; experiencing the discomfort it causes and examining why the trigger and anxiety are connected. Then my therapist will try to break the association, often by bringing something completely ridiculous in ... It's kind of like in the Harry Potter books and how they deal with 'boggarts'. The boggart turns into your worst fear and the way to defeat it is to turn the image into something funny that doesn't scare you.

These therapies aren't DPD-specific but they can definitely be of benefit, especially to those struggling with emotional problems and self-esteem issues. Plus, they're all pretty readily available.

Another area of treatment people often ask about is medication. When it comes to DPD-specific treatment plans at least, drugs are rarely used on their own – they're supplementary to the psychological therapy. As part of my initial Maudsley assessment, I was trialled on the most common combinations of drugs you tend to find in the treatment of DPD: a selective serotonin reuptake inhibitor (SSRI) antidepressant (for me, sertraline) and lamotrigine (an epilepsy med that's now more widely used in mental health services as a mood stabilizer). Professor David explains:

> We investigated lamotrigine because it blocks the depersonalization-like effects of ketamine when used experimentally. We subsequently found that the combination of lamotrigine and an antidepressant seems to be better than either alone, but really rigorous clinical trials have not been done.

This pairing is often the starting point for exploring medications. Despite the limited trials, it's the only combination that has shown any degree of statistical success, although in reality the percentage of people it helps is still low. It didn't have any effect on me, and aside from it making me need the toilet several times during the night, I didn't feel anything different despite being on the maximum dose of both. When I was coming off the sertraline, I did encounter brain zaps – common for SSRI withdrawal, and in hindsight that's probably what my 'brain electrocuting me' was on the Prozac (fluoxetine) years ago. They feel grim, but ultimately aren't dangerous.

Other medications can sometimes be trialled but they're typically off-licence for the condition and are used on a more experimental basis. I've heard of various other SSRIs, serotonin–norepinephrine reuptake inhibitors (SNRIs) and tricyclic antidepressants, anti-anxiety meds (e.g. diazepam, benzodiazepines), psychological stimulants (e.g. modafinil), anti-psychotics (e.g. trifluoperazine, olanzapine) and others all being trialled. For a while I was put on naltrexone, a medication that aids withdrawal from opioids or alcohol, but studies have been done trialling it for DPD specifically. Basically, it counteracts the numbing effect of those substances, and for some can relieve the emotional numbing of DPD. Again, it had no positive effect on me: I had to have fortnightly blood tests as it's metabolized by the liver, and after a few months I had to withdraw from it entirely as my alanine aminotransferase (ALT) levels went through the roof, indicating my liver was taking a beating.

Accessing medications is completely dependent on finding a clinician willing to prescribe them – I've been told before that for off-licence meds, it's usually an 'on their head be it' situation if anything were to go wrong, so many clinicians are reluctant to experiment. Again, there is no medication known to 'cure' depersonalization, and although some people may get relief from a particular med, or it might improve their mental health in other areas, which then has a corresponding effect on the depersonalization, almost all trials have shown no statistical evidence that any are effective for DPD on a wider scale. The likes of antidepressants are palliative treatments – they don't address the root causes, they just mask the symptoms. Plus, some medications can make depersonalization worse – either through the anxiety of taking them or their effects mirroring the sensations. In the Alastair Campbell documentary (2019) mentioned in Chapter 4, he explains, 'I've been on antidepressants for years. I've tried several different types, and definitely felt their side effects...tiredness, feeling lethargic, and feeling numbed. That sense sometimes that you're not quite there.'

Considering the possible side effects of medications and whether they're worth the risk is very important. Naltrexone did my liver in; lamotrigine comes with the (statistically low) possibility of Stevens–Johnson Syndrome, a severe skin reaction that can be fatal; and a medication I was on once upon a time (I forget which) detailed the potential side effect of 'death' as *sixth* on the list. It might make logical sense to trial a certain med if a clinician suspects it might help the underlying cause of your DPD, but the odds do need to be weighed up. I don't like the idea of using mind-altering medications. My willingness to be a pharmaceutical guinea pig nowadays is simply born of desperation.

A treatment that has made a few waves in recent years is Repetitive Transcranial Magnetic Stimulation (rTMS), primarily because studies that were done specifically into its effectiveness on primary DPD 'showed promise' (Hunter *et al.* 2017). It's important not to confuse this with Electroconvulsive Therapy (ECT), the so-called 'electro-shock treatment' that's often depicted in psychological thrillers. As the name suggests, rTMS works by administering magnetism rather than electricity – so although the two treatments might look and sound similar, they're very different. Professor David is responsible for a lot of the research that has taken place into this as a potential treatment for DPD:

> rTMS has been tried as a treatment with some effect but only in very small uncontrolled trials. Our work has targeted the ventrolateral pre-frontal cortex [VLPFC] – one of the areas which might be 'suppressing' activity in 'emotional' parts of the brain. So, if rTMS can 'dial down' activity in the VLPFC it may improve symptoms. Again, there is some preliminary support for this, but not controlled studies. The good thing about rTMS is that it does not have permanent effects and has few side effects.

The therapy works by passing pulses from an electromagnetic coil through the skull and using them to directly stimulate or suppress specific areas of the brain that might be responsible for certain mental health conditions. It's most commonly used for depression; but in the case of DPD, if the VLPFC has too much authority over the emotional regulation system and is keeping everything suppressed unnecessarily, using rTMS to reduce activity in that area of the brain would – theoretically – allow the amygdala and insula to light up more than the VLPFC was allowing them to before, as well as reducing our tendencies towards obsessive thought patterns. It's a bit of a seesaw effect: you push the front down and the back is able to ping back up, making the whole system more equally balanced, and in turn, better emotionally regulated and with greater interoception. That's the theory, anyway.

In addition to this, Dr Simeon found that brain scans on DPD patients showed increased activity in the right temporoparietal junction (TPJ): an area of the brain that contributes to 'self–other differentiation' (Eddy 2016). Trials then suggested that suppressing this area could also have a positive effect on depersonalization. Both the VLPFC and TPJ can be targeted during rTMS therapy. If a patient doesn't respond to the former, the latter can be tried.

Having gone through a full course of the treatment for both depression and DPD, dodie explains what the experience was like:

> You get set up with a cap that protects your head, and they find the part they want to focus on. For me, they focused on the part for depression and two points for DPD. They do a test to see what your threshold is, on a point that affects your motor functions, and they go up until your hand twitches - that's your limit. Then, you just lie there for ages. They put a heavy magnet on your head and there's this loud click every second or so. It might make your jaw twitch because it's near some muscles. They said I might notice a difference after the first or second session. I was so hopeful, imagining my new life! But I didn't see any difference in my depersonalization symptoms. I was so upset. That being said, in terms of depression it was genuinely helpful - I felt such a difference. After my sessions I'd walk out dancing down the road!

dodie's rTMS not helping her DPD does again reinforce the fact that everybody is different when it comes to treatment – although some patients in studies responded to it, it didn't have any effect on others. Private UK treatment company Smart TMS say on their website that 'in some cases, we don't see any improvements so the decision to try TMS to treat your Depersonalization Disorder is an individual one'. Further, they sent me literature detailing that they've so far treated 21 patients with DPD, of whom three 'went into remission' – defined by Smart TMS as having their Cambridge Depersonalization Scale score move below 70. It's important to consider, though, that we don't know how far above that threshold the patients were originally, and whether dipping below 70 was due to the rTMS or external factors; and equally, whether the other 86 per cent of patients had some improvement, or none at all.

I would agree that trying rTMS therapy is definitely a personal choice: the odds of potential benefits need to be weighed up against the cost. It can be difficult to access it affordably, with patients typically having to use private companies to administer it. In the USA, the Mayo clinics and Pulse TMS both offer it and in the UK it is available via the likes of the Priory clinics. Although in 2017 it was reported that it was available on the NHS (but not specifically for DPD) in two NHS trusts (Tracey 2017), whether this limited provision has expanded since then is unclear. Courses of treatment typically run into many thousands of pounds, making it unaffordable for most, but price-wise it's competitive with private psychological therapy. I'm not wanting to discourage you from trying rTMS if it's an option for you – I would jump at the opportunity if finances allowed – but again, expectations do need to be realistic.

There are some more 'out there' (i.e. they are definitely not considered mainstream) treatments beginning to circulate. I need to stress that I'm absolutely not trying to endorse these, nor should they ever be done illegally. However, in recent years, researchers have been investigating the potential of psilocybin (the psychoactive chemical in magic mushrooms) in treating mental health conditions. Studies so far have again focused on depression, and, as we know, that can feed into DPD. In her 2017 TED talk, Imperial College London researcher Dr Rosalind Watts discussed a controlled trial of 20 patients with treatment-resistant depression who were given psilocybin: 11 found their symptoms greatly reduced for two months; and six were still in complete remission six months afterwards. In the talk, Dr Watts explained:

> So many of the patients described feeling numb and unable to feel. Many of them had described experiencing trauma in their lives, often in early childhood, and they'd never been able to process it or think about what had happened.

(Sound familiar?) The patients described the experience of being given psilocybin as, 'like when you defrag a hard drive' and 'like a fog lifting'. This is all in relation to depression and processing trauma, but the commonalities are clear. Unlike antidepressants though, it's thought the psilocybin helps to guide the patient through resolving their core problems rather than just applying a pharmaceutical sticking plaster.

Dr Watts later described the patients' progress:

> After that mental reboot, they were able to connect to their senses, connect to themselves, their identity ... They went from being trapped to being unlocked, expanded and free ... I believe that if we incorporate psilocybin into existing short-term therapies, we can make them so

much more effective. It's supplementing therapy with a medicine that lets you find a way out of your suffering, rather than just padding the cage.

The research is very much in its infancy and, as I said, I'm not trying to encourage you to pursue it, but it's certainly an interesting alternative angle to think about. I've often said to therapists that I feel my sense of unreality is now so extreme that talking therapies have proven ineffective as they rely on you being able to 'internalize' what's discussed. For me, I've gone to the sessions, I've (to steal one of Jane's wonderful expressions) 'made all the right noises' and then left feeling like it all never happened. Nothing ever 'goes in', so to speak. If psilocybin could (metaphorically) break down the wall surrounding my mind and allow processing to occur, I think I would try it. However, it would only ever be in a controlled environment, under the supervision of professionals, and somewhere that it's legal. Currently, the only places able to offer such treatments are clinics in Holland (e.g. Synthesis). I wouldn't be against looking into it further.

After all the psychological therapies I've had, I think there's a very important message that often gets missed. I spoke earlier about the frustrations of therapies often being viewed as 'absolutes' rather than links in a chain – which is true in public health services especially – but assuming the treatment has a positive effect, it's somewhat meant to be like that. As someone once said to me, 'Therapy doesn't end when therapy ends.' The taught techniques are still relevant after the sessions are over. I continued my 'successes diary' for months after I was discharged from the Maudsley and I still add to it on occasion now. It's important to remember that the teachings of therapy are long-term solutions; even though the sessions are finite.

It's definitely been a comfort to understand that people can and do recover from long-term, chronic DPD after many years –it's easy to forget that in the depths of our suffering. Recovery doesn't necessarily mean that the symptoms have gone entirely, but patients are better able to cope with them and have them impact their lives much less. Dr Hunter elaborates:

> With most people it's a slow fade out – it's not a quick drop. There are some people who will have moments where it completely drops, but from my experience those are often people for whom it's very transient ... although there are people where it's been a sudden 'off' and it's stayed off for years. When we've analysed the figures from the last five years' worth of data [from therapy], we've seen a dialling down of the intensity of depersonalization. People aren't always getting to absolute zero. For some people the symptoms don't always change that much, although they usually do. It's rare for people not to show any decline, but they understand it and it's having less impact on their life and functioning. [However] I have had people where they literally have no symptoms any more – but it is hard to predict that.

I occasionally get messages from people regarding their recoveries – usually something along the lines of 'I was cured of depersonalization, but it's come back. Was I not cured properly?' We need to remember that reducing or 'getting rid' of depersonalization symptoms is possible, but when that occurs, it doesn't stop depersonalization being your in-built psychological defence mechanism. It doesn't erase the program from our hard drive; it just means we've closed – or minimized – the window. If we then go through another difficult time, and the stressors pile up again, our mind can feel the need to re-trigger the response – that's the nature of it being reactionary.

So, if it comes and then goes, that isn't a guarantee you'll never experience it ever again – you've not gained 'immunity', as it were. What seems to make the real difference longer term, if you already have a propensity towards depersonalizing, is giving yourself the psychological toolkit to recognize it, understand it and control it.

Somebody who had such an experience is Tom. He endured two separate periods of chronic depersonalization. He recovered naturally from the first one (which occurred when he was 21 and lasted 2–3 years), but when it came back at the age of 30, it was just as unbearable as before. He recalls:

> With it came these horrible feelings of 'I just don't know if I've got the energy to go through getting better again.

However, recognizing he needed professional help, Tom began several years of therapy with a specialist. Over time, he was slowly able to understand what was happening and reduce the hold his DPD had over him, to the point where he is now completely free of symptoms and able to live a very fruitful and contented life. He says:

> My therapist was able to help me permanently change my relationship with the condition. Depersonalization tries to trick you into making you feel as though you're not there, and not real ... It takes some excavation to realize that you are. I have genuinely switched it off. It's in my mind and I can turn it on and feel it. But what has changed profoundly is my relationship with that experience and this is what 'recovery' is for me. It's allowed me to get on and live a happy life. I might have an unexpected reminder of it a couple of times a year and suddenly feel the sensation, but thanks to the tools I learned in therapy, it's fleeting and moments

later I am moving on with my day. It took years to get there, but I really do feel free of depersonalization.

... The big thing was realizing that the condition - the physiological experience of the depersonalization - was one thing, but the whole architecture of terror, doubt, alienation, fear and anxiety around it was a different thing. There were always little relapses; but after that moment, it lost all its power and I could see it for what it was. The moment I stopped giving it attention and being scared of it, I found its power diminished quite rapidly. I learned its true nature - and that allowed me to move on.

This is a story I've heard from many who have been on that journey. Their recovery might not have completely taken away their symptoms, but what really changed is how they understand the condition and interact with it. If the fear of experiencing depersonalization is what the depersonalization is ultimately trying to protect you from, for example, breaking that cycle of terror and understanding *why* your mind is reacting that way has been the key to taking away its hold. This won't be the case for everybody - so far, I'm proof of that. Recovery is not usually an easy process, especially for long-term DPD. However, we should never give up hope, because it's possible and absolutely does happen.

11.
#Existing

Technology and DPD

I've always had a love–hate relationship with technology. I'm just about old enough to remember what life was like before we all had computers, but, in a way, 'devices' and I have grown up together. Coming from a musical background, even when younger I was of the opinion that digital technologies were the enemy. Having to make records on a computer felt like I was cheating, and that the music I was producing was somehow invalid because of it. But the more I've thought it through, the more I've realized technology isn't the enemy at all – it's incredible; and the benefits hugely outweigh any shortcomings. The enemy, I think, is what the technology tricks us into doing with it.

Stripped back to its basic elements, digital tech is such a powerful innovation and has revolutionized everything. In terms of DPD specifically, so many people I've spoken to have said they wouldn't have known they had it without the internet – and I include myself in that sentiment. I'd probably still be sat in primary care appointments discussing herbal teas if it hadn't been for finding that *Guardian* newspaper article (Swains 2015) online. Self-diagnosing and hoping the experts agree is the 'place' most of us have come from, and finding others like ourselves in public forums and Facebook groups gives us much-needed validation and support. Alina says:

> At this point in time they are lot more helpful than the treatment many of us have received from mental health providers who were uneducated about DPD.

Without the internet, equipping ourselves with knowledge about our condition would be nigh on impossible. Jen adds:

> One night I turned to Twitter and used it as a search engine for depersonalization and derealization. I was amazed at what came up and how many people were tweeting about their experiences. Others were describing symptoms but didn't know what they were.

In terms of the work of the Unreal charity, so much of what we do is online and through social media – responding to comments and signposting people to relevant resources, providing virtual peer support groups, sharing infographics to raise awareness on social media, etc. We couldn't do what we do if the world wasn't online.

There's something very cathartic about discussing our problems with fellow sufferers, because it's one of the only times we can bin the metaphors and cut the crap. We don't need to explain ourselves, because the other person already 'gets it'; we can skip that whole rigmarole and get straight to more important matters. I'd urge anybody with lived experience of the condition – sufferers, carers, parents, friends – to find an online community to explore. You can learn so much, and engaging with others can be reassuring from both sides of the equation. As I said earlier, you need to look after yourself and only enter that world when you're in the right frame of mind to do so, but I really would encourage it overall.

All that said though, I do think we need to be very careful with technology, especially in relation to our mental health. Without careful management and awareness of what it's capable of, it can quickly control and consume us. It makes us do things not because we need to but just because we can. It can be very coercive in telling us that unless we keep up with it, we'll become irrelevant or forgotten about. Gimmicks have become necessities, and many digital products are developed to directly trigger our basic psychological needs, such as giving 'feeds' no natural end point so we find them addictive and can't stop swiping. Photoshop filters give us the means to create 'perfection' from less-than-perfect source material. As one online culture magazine put it, 'It is less the technology, more the changes in behaviour it enables that causes problems' (Burke 2019).

An area of the modern digital world we're all *au fait* with is social media, and it really is wonderful in so many ways. Especially during Covid-19, being able to share content virtually has been a lifeline that's made enforced separation bearable for so many. However, I really do think it does way more harm than good when looking at its wider effects on our psychology and society. I know it's trendy nowadays to bash it – I'm not trying to jump on the tabloid '*anti*social media' bandwagon, but I do think a big problem is that the 'reality' it presents can be so biased.

When we interact with tech that gives us a choice of how we portray ourselves, we inevitably give extra consideration to how our words and photographs might be perceived by others – it's going back to what we discussed with Dr Ciaunica about seeing ourselves from a third-person perspective (Chapter 5). As a result, we create a digital persona – which is essentially who we are. But we can manipulate how others see us, in much the same way as politicians try to do, by being selective with what we share. We tend to shout about the peaks and be much quieter about the troughs. You'll be more likely to write something on Twitter when you pass an exam with flying colours than when your dog dies, for example. We all have that one friend we 'unfollow' because they're a black hole of positivity.

The macro effect of this is that when we look at a 'timeline', we're presented with a very filtered perception of what others' lives are like. Yes, it's rooted in reality, but it's an enhanced reality, with the surface noise removed. As Dr Bezzubova writes, "'I' of Facebook or Match.com is an image that represents not a particular person as she is, but this person's hopes, wishes, fantasies or intentions' (2018). You only see the good bits, and comparing our own real life to that can make us feel inadequate. Sitting on the bus home from work and swiping through a feed, you'll see people on holiday, buying new cars and going to festivals, but probably won't hear about bereavements, redundancies or evictions. Perhaps, most importantly, it won't reassure you that millions of other people are also sat on a sweaty bus feeling equally as disgruntled with the world as you are.

This highlight-reel nature of social media has a nasty habit of playing on our insecurities. Even when we're aware of how filtered it is, it still somehow bypasses our rationality, reinforcing negative self-beliefs that we're not interesting or valued and making us feel like we're the only ones who are struggling. Unless it's your turn to be the one peacocking the exciting news, these websites rarely make you feel better about how your life is going, especially when you're battling a mental health issue. We cannot help but treat the staged perfection as a mirror, but then when we don't like the reflection, our mood drops.

I refer to this psychology as '#Existing' (or 'Hashtag Existing', if for you '#' still denotes a phone number). It's the mentality that unless something is broadcast online, it hasn't really happened. You need to leave a constant virtual paper trail. If you can't provide your friends with regular evidence that you're still alive, then they'd probably best just forget you. Even if the updates are so banal it hurts, it's a routine you must get into to maintain relevance. Every photograph of somebody's lunchtime burger seems to grimace, 'Ate some food today: I need it to survive. #Existing.'

The climate of social media has definitely changed for us over the past decade. What began as a positive means of connecting with others has grown massively and taken on more worrying undertones. Gerald – a journalist – explains:

> It's almost like we've undergone this early optimism and excite-ment of having the world's knowledge in your pocket. But around 2010, I think the culture began to get a sense of the sinister aspects of social media, which now everyone is aware of ... Tech companies are on the defence now.

When the early forms of this technology emerged in the 2000s – which for me was Bebo and MSN Messenger – it created another problem. Up to that point I only had to endure bullying during school hours, but then the tech allowed the bullies to follow me home. This was a time before smartphones, so they could only get me when I was sat at my computer. Nowadays, there is literally no escape as notifications are delivered to us, regardless of time or location.

It's not just confined to vindictive people who know us though. The ability for strangers to hurl abuse whilst shielded by virtual anonymity is a problem people of all ages experience on public platforms. I've never had it *too* bad – I've only received one death threat in my years on YouTube (over having a soft toy whale on my bed...can you imagine?!) – but others have it so much worse. Stories are always hitting the press about individuals taking their own lives following cyberbullying and 'trolls' who do their best to push others over the edge with cruelty. You only have to watch the BBC documentary on what Little Mix's Jesy Nelson endured following her *X-Factor* appearances to see how bad things can get, especially when you're in the public eye: 'My brain started to believe everything that people were saying about me' (2019). It's really no surprise that children subjected to abuse online are twice as likely to self-harm or attempt suicide (Knapton 2018), yet half of ten-year-olds in the UK now own a smartphone that enables online abuse to happen (Kleinman 2020).

The issue of overstimulation is another area where having the world at our fingertips isn't always a good thing. Engaging with technology is now the primary way we occupy ourselves during downtime – hence the adverts on television warning parents to enforce a healthy 'screen time balance' with their kids. Integrative psychotherapist Hilda Burke says, 'When we're bored, we look at our phones. Fifty years ago, that might have been a space for random associations, thoughts, creativity, or just being bored. I think a lot of us use our smartphones as a kind of pacifier, to avoid boredom' (2019). The internet gives us access to so much more information than ever before, but often we see what's pushed at us by algorithms rather than what we actively search for, so we're exposed to things we might not want to see. Heather adds:

I genuinely think social media is destroying people's lives. In relation to mental health it can be a very negative thing, not least because it makes us all far too aware of everything that is going on in the world, which can be very overwhelming.

Keeping abreast of current affairs is important, but being reminded of them constantly can magnify how much we worry about them. This can absolutely feed into DPD directly. Neuroscientist Dr Patrick McNamara writes: 'Dissociative experiences may in turn be linked to an influx, from internal and external sources, of too much information. The cognitive system becomes overwhelmed' (2013). If we're already going through a difficult time and our cognitive load is high, filling our minds with surplus content that's likely to stress us out and 'clog' things up can certainly nudge us further towards the threshold of dissociation. Another study investigated the impact social media usage had on employees in a work environment, and noted that those 'who have a low level of mindfulness are those who suffer from social media use at work; as the intensity of social media use increases, they tend to experience higher emotional exhaustion and depersonalization' (Charoensukmongkol 2015, p.1974). With mindfulness defined as 'the quality of being present and fully engaged' (Headspace), which of course is lacking in DPD, it could be argued that using social media whilst depersonalized might potentially exacerbate our condition specifically.

There was also an interesting study done at Oxford University into the effects of social media on adolescent paranoia. One of the findings there was that 'problematic social media use was instead a consequence of existing psychological and social difficulties ... Paranoid fears activate these threat-focused cognitive processes that in turn bias threatening appraisals of social content' (Bird et al. 2018, p.1140). Social media can feel like a refuge for people struggling with isolation and their mental health, which can then lead to excessive use. However, using it whilst we're in a bad place can make us compare ourselves even more unfavourably to others and leave us feeling worse than if we'd engaged with it in a better state of mind. As dodie explains:

> I think it's getting worse. I used to love it, it used to be so valuable to me, especially in all my struggles. But now, I think it's grown to the point where there's too many voices, and I find myself looking at myself through the lens of somebody who's judging me, and who hates me already, because that's how a lot of the internet will act. I think a lot of the time it feeds this self-hatred ... People often say in interviews, 'You're so open online!', but I'm not anymore; I'm really not. And I feel so much better for it – it feels so good to keep stuff private. It's hard, because I feel people almost wanting to get in, because I used to share that much ... It's hard dealing with boundaries.

Like many others, I went along with social media as it emerged, for fear of being forgotten about, whilst feeling uncomfortable with how compelled I felt to broadcast my life. I hated the pageantry of it. Facebook Messenger is one of the main ways people communicate though, so not to be on Facebook would be unthinkable.

But then came a bit of a breakthrough. I realized all my friends know my phone number. They know where I live. I have a website with my email address on it. A Google search throws up my YouTube. I'm not exactly hard to find. I was making *DPD Diaries* videos about how I felt social media was damaging our mental health, but by being on Facebook, Twitter and Instagram, I was as much a part of the whole thing as everybody else. A few hours beforehand I'd hidden the apps on my phone – and despite being somebody who

I'd have said didn't really use them, I still found myself mindlessly going to 'check the socials' with alarming regularity. I was addicted to getting my phone out of my pocket and thumbing that big blue 'F', even though I genuinely wasn't bothered about its contents. As soon as the apps were gone, I saw just how bad the problem was. I simply couldn't stop myself springing for those now-empty spaces on the screen.

One Sunday in 2018, I decided to be a conscientious objector and delete all of my personal social media. Gone. Facebook told me they thought I'd be back. Not a chance. I wanted out. I was done. Deleting the spectacle I'd reluctantly engaged with for all these years finally felt like something I could realistically do.

I can say with complete honesty that I've not once missed any of it. Removing it from my life has been such a breath of fresh air. I still find out what my friends have been up to if they want to tell me, but the fog of unnecessary opinions and pictures of other people's pets I'd been cluttering my brain with is gone. I no longer spend big chunks of my day reading about all the 'life progress' other people have been making and feeling horrendous that I'm still living at home in adulthood like some budget Principal Skinner from *The Simpsons*. Comparing ourselves to others is dangerous enough at the best of times.

I'm not saying you should take such drastic measures as I did, but I'd encourage you to think about how – and how often – you engage with all this technology. Yes, it's wonderful in so many ways. Yes, it has obvious benefits. Zoom kept the world running during Covid-19. And I'm certainly not suggesting you should isolate your-self unnecessarily – that's never good. But technology should serve us, not control us. A huge part of our problem with DPD is feeling removed from reality, and pouring more and more of ourselves into the synthetic digital haze is never going to help us regain control of that. We need to be living in the moment, not in the trend. We need to get out of the virtual world and back in touch with the real one. This is our unreality check.

12.
Perspectives

I've never been any good at ending things succinctly. Whenever I try to wrap up a YouTube video it reminds me of when I saw Bryan Adams and he played five encores – he just wouldn't go away. But given everything we've discussed, I thought a sensible way to end this whole journey might be to take a step back and reflect on a few of the most important things that I feel need highlighting about the condition. I've spoken to many professionals, each with a unique view that really brought new ideas to the fore. Patterns have emerged, and seemingly unrelated areas were all fundamentally saying the same things. I wanted to leave you with three messages that I think are the most important takeaways about depersonalization, primarily from the perspective of a sufferer, but more generally also.

First: Depersonalization – both episodic and chronic – is a reaction to another problem. It's not a disease; it's a defence mechanism. For those who experience it transiently (e.g. during times of panic), the depersonalization is your mind trying to protect you from the distress of that experience. As Dr Hunter says, 'Depersonalization is trying to be your friend.' It feels horrible, but it's not permanent.

Recovery is typically swift once the stressors causing the response subside. The mind doesn't feel it needs to protect you anymore and the depersonalization releases its hold.

Chronic DPD, as a primary diagnosis, is a completely different experience for everybody, including root causes, triggers, perpetuating factors, treatment, coping strategies and recovery. There is no 'cure' in terms of one thing being universally effective. Recovery is dependent on identifying the specific factors that are driving it for *you*. Once those are addressed and brought more under control, or the thought patterns and behaviours are adjusted into more healthy ones, the depersonalization *should* slowly fade out, a bit like house lights on a dimmer switch. Despite being present much longer term, harder to treat and embedded in the core of who we are, the experience is still fundamentally reactionary. Our mind is trying to help us cope.

Second: I really do think that some of the underlying reasons for DPD – and many other mental health conditions – can be partly cultural, even if it then takes something more individualized to ultimately trigger it. As so many social commentators have highlighted, our culture has shifted in a way that isn't good for our collective mental health. Johann Hari compares the emphases of a capitalist society to junk food: 'junk values' (2019). Entrepreneur Tom Savage explains how 'the greatest minds of our generation now spend their days trying to work out how to make people click on more adverts' (2015). And technologies reducing our interactions with other human beings – from online helpdesk 'chatbots' to self-service supermarket checkouts – are everywhere. Our obsession with digital automation is cutting jobs at a time when we need to be creating them. And with tech geniuses using technology to prod at our insecurities, our collective mental health is deteriorating.

One of the real eye-openers during my research was Dr Guralnik explaining – unprompted – how DPD can be rooted in a mismatch within our socio-political identity. I'd often suspected it, but she was the first to say it to me specifically. It's the idea of having a fundamental element of *who you are* that you're at odds with, especially in a cultural sense; something that might be causing a friction within your sense of self. Elaborating on her point, she added:

> A person can feel some sort of mismatch with their social milieu that causes a deep experience of depersonalization, and there's no way to narrate it without addressing those dimensions. It can be on any dimension: class, ethnicity, religion ... Just some kind of misalignment with one's collective.

The idea of a disparity deep within us being something that potentially triggers the protective reflex is both fascinating and terrifying. Psychiatrist and trauma expert Dr Richard Loewenstein explains that 'ego psychology – theories of conflict – are extraordinarily important in understanding these patients [of dissociation]' (2018). And psychoanalytic theories dating back many decades suggest that DPD can be 'a defense mechanism to protect the ego from internally generated psychodynamic conflicts' (Hunter, Salkovskis and David 2013, pp.20–21). I'm an introvert but one who wishes he was recognized by others as having achieved something significant. I have a desire to be a *name* yet I am simultaneously so thankful that nobody really knows it. Are those just harmless quirks of my personality or the root of this whole problem? Yale psychiatrist Dr James Charney described in an article for the *Washington Post* that depersonalization sufferers are often egodystonic: 'The patient becomes alien to their ideal self-image, which is crippling and can destroy their life and those around them' (cited in Dunne 2019). A little dramatic perhaps but this does suggest that when our ambitions and reality don't align, the tension can cause us to dissociate. Perhaps this is a consequence of a culture that encourages everybody to dream big and aim high? Some people 'make it', but for those of us who don't, the reality of our self-image becomes estranged from who we wish it had become and it creates an internal friction.

Third: The global lack of awareness surrounding DPD is even more appalling than I first thought. I knew doctors failing to diagnose us was 'the' story, but everybody, the whole world over, has such similar pathways to treatment, even within more specialist secondary and tertiary care sectors. In addition, the unbearable grind of trying to get *anywhere* at all in mental health services can contribute to our mental health deteriorating further. On this subject, dodie explains:

> The doctor basically said, 'You've been quite busy. I think it's dangerous to diagnose someone with a mental health condition so young. You've been up and about – if you're well enough to do that, you're probably alright.' ... It made me feel so embarrassed and silly, like I was wrong. I didn't go back to the doctor's about it for years – and in those years, I spiralled *so* hard because I felt like I was going mad.

We've got to stop this from being the norm. Medical professionals treating struggling, vulnerable people with contempt when we try to explain what *we know* is going on is the worst thing to come up against. After explaining her symptoms to a psychologist, Mara says:

> He looked pretty amused – as if I was audaciously self-diagnosing with some exotic disorder that wasn't on his list.

I think we're often viewed as the know-it-all hypochondriacs who spend too much time on Google and self-diagnose ourselves with whatever happens to be top of the search results that day. No, we don't; and, as a professional, admitting you're not sure what's wrong with somebody and referring them to somebody who might, should not be something that bruises professional pride. Nobody knows everything; and especially with how little training frontline doctors get about mental health, accepting a problem is beyond your remit and passing the case to an expert in that field should be actively encouraged, not a reluctant last resort decades down the line. As Dr Černis explains:

> Within mental health specialties, there's little or no training on dissociation – on my psychology training course, there was nothing. So, I think there's the 'top-down' problem of the information from training not being there. But there's also a 'bottom-up' difficulty of it being something that's so hard to describe that people either try and are misunderstood, realize they're not getting anywhere and stop, or they never try. So, there's two halves of silence.

We need both those halves to speak up.

I mentioned in Chapter 5 about the bittersweet experience of hearing 'Everlong' at Foo Fighters' gigs. I stood in the crowd at Glastonbury 2017 as they ended the show with it. As fireworks exploded out of the top of the stage and illuminated the night sky to screams of joy from the 100,000 other sweaty people lost in the moment, and feeling faint pangs of emotion behind my eyes trying to break out but not being able to, I remember thinking to myself that DPD affects 1 per cent of the population (let's be optimistic). In that crowd, a thousand people were feeling the same way as I was. *A thousand*. In one field. And yet, we could all go home, describe our symptoms to a GP and be told to take a nice hot bath. How the hell is that right?

There's so much more work to be done. But, I hope this book goes on to become a tiny part of the movement towards there being a smoother ride for people who develop these debilitating symptoms – even if that's just arming more individuals with the knowledge needed to convince a single healthcare professional of the disorder's existence. We need to bring the fight for greater awareness from every conceivable angle, regardless of how small they might seem.

To close, I wanted to give my fellow sufferers the final say. You've heard my thoughts on everything; but what about everybody else? I asked my DPD friends what *they* would most like people to know about their condition, and their situations.

Before treatment for DPD I lived an isolated life. I had lost the sense of who I was. I endured severe depression and anxiety, coupled with complex physical health issues. Being unable to connect to my core values of helping others I existed in a lonely bubble where I would go through external processes with no empathy. It was as if I was someone else who I was watching from above me. I was a prisoner in my own house as DPD had contributed to me constantly experiencing non-epileptic seizures that left me afraid when I was on my own, exhausted and unable to get myself home. Losing awareness of the speed and distance of cars impacted my ability to cross roads and perform simple tasks like going to buy a pint of milk or a bar of chocolate. I would sit and ruminate on negative thoughts for hours on end.

CBT gave me the strength, space and confidence to examine my mind, put ear worms into context and slowly reconnect my brain's fragmented pathways. With help and patience, I have found new ways to achieve and live a lifestyle that still reflects the old me and my values. But it is the new me that I am now with DPD; not ruled by it. Discovering that I wasn't alone with my symptoms and meeting other people who have lived experience of DPD helped me to demystify it. With support from my therapist, DPD has lost its scary hold on me. My physical and emotional symptoms still come but I now have an understanding of why it's happening and a 'box of tricks' to enable me to work with it when it rears its ugly head. I can now concentrate on living my life rather than feeling that I exist in a vacuum.

Lin

Finding out that all these seemingly random and unconnected symptoms were actually manifestations of one disorder was a real revelation. Before, it felt like someone had mixed the pieces of many different puzzles and I had to somehow solve them all at once, without even knowing how many puzzles there were. Suddenly, I realized that all these pieces are actually part of one big puzzle. Even though putting them together was hard, it was nowhere near as hard as before. I felt I now could focus on understanding this condition and why it translates into each of these symptoms. For other well-researched and well-understood conditions, this isn't a process people have to go through. I think this is the one thing I wish people knew about, as this would help them appreciate the long, confusing journey people have been through, which often exacerbates their symptoms and makes it even harder to connect with others.

Meeting others who have been through this extremely lonely journey was a crucial moment in my life. Being fortunate enough to be functioning normally in society meant my friends and family couldn't appreciate how lost and confused I felt deep inside, despite looking perfectly fine on the outside. Before meeting others, and even after finding a name for my condition, I often questioned whether I really had it, mirroring the way others were seeing me. But this only led me to more loneliness. Meeting others helped me to realize that I really have it, made it real for me and helped me embrace all aspects of myself as well as stop questioning my perception of this experience. The instant connection I felt with these people I met was deeply profound as it was based on sharing an experience that I thought no-one else had before. Being a gay man, I often compare it to the process of coming out as gay in terms of feeling accepted and comfortable with your own self.

Andreas

It is completely surreal and terrifying. I have felt and experienced things that literally seem completely out of this world. It's like someone stealing you from inside your body. It's left as a shell, but you can still function, and people expect you to be the same. It's so hard for others to understand, but they just need to trust what we say.

Focusing on what you can do and not what you can no longer do is really important. The hardest thing is that others see you the same. For me I have fundamentally 'gone': the person I was disappeared, and I felt like I was just my body, with no sense of self. Yet, others just see you the same and expect you to carry on as normal. Invisible illnesses are so disabling and isolating. You learn to lower your expectations of yourself and of others.

It's not a choice. None of us have chosen to have this. We must adapt and accept things and we need support from others around us to do the same. It's like we have lost a 'sense' - and in the same way that if we had lost hearing, sight, etc., we need support. We cannot just think our way out of it. Thinking positively does not stop DPD, just like it doesn't stop cancer. Yes, positivity is a huge help, but it is not a cure.

Jen

It's so bad; and sometimes I'm like, 'There's no way I'm living with this; I hate it so much.' I would do anything - *anything* - to get rid of it. I'd rather cut off a limb. I'd rather be sick every day. I'd take anything. But, I have it. And if I have it, I have to find some kind of good in it, because if I don't, I'll just go mad. So, being able to give it a purpose of spreading the word and learning about mental health, I've gained so much empathy from having this.

The biggest thing that's helped has been learning to get over my depression that was caused by the DPD. I refused to believe that I could live life with it. I would not stop until it was gone, and only then could I not be depressed. But what actually happened was I found a way to prove to myself that I didn't need to feel depressed with this. It fucking sucks - and don't get me wrong, I definitely still feel the depression sometimes - but having it constantly and telling [my]self 'Listen, I'm just going to do my best, live my life with this the best I can, and take what I can get' has really helped a lot. Just accepting that I have it has helped my overall mood.

I'll never stop trying, even though I've accepted I have it, and this is my life now. It's just different. It sucks sometimes; it's okay others. But I'll still always try.

dodie

There is still a big stigma around mental illness in Germany, and mental health is seldom discussed in public. This includes my own family. Since there was no known mental illness on either side of my family, there were never any discussions about mental health. Over the years, whenever I would bring up feeling overwhelmed or stressed by school or university, my parents would immediately tell me to 'pull myself together' and 'power through'. They did not understand the constant fear and stress I felt, so I no longer attempted to talk about my struggles.

However, they did notice the consequences my symptoms had on my life and frequently complained about my declining academic performance. Feeling unreal and disconnected from my body and the world around me caused me to lose interest in the people and hobbies I used to love. I never felt like I could properly describe my experience, so I didn't. The fear I could be losing my mind and going mad further stopped me from reaching out to others. After discovering the terms 'derealization' and 'depersonalization', I finally felt able to explain my situation.

Alina

This is just my idiosyncrasy, but I'd say the most important thing has been the difference between acceptance and 'true acceptance'. In my case, I've had to truly accept that I'm going to live a life - at least in part, and for now - that is sub-par. I've had to let go of the idea that I'm going to feel 100 per cent, and learn that it's okay to be semi-functional. It's been coming to an understanding that even though people around us now are talking, and it's something of a vibrant atmosphere, we have no idea what's going on internally in their lives. The apparent happiness we're observing could conceal a completely different story. Basics like that were really helpful for me; [plus the thought] that even if I was feeling at 30 per cent one day rather than 60 per cent or 80 per cent, I could still live a life that was worthy.

Gerald

Part of the reason I started getting interested in mental health was because I grew up in this neighbourhood which had a hugely high suicide rate among teenagers, and the CDC [Centers for Disease Control and Prevention] came in to investigate. I grew up in the super-affluent Silicon Valley - the home of Google, Apple and Facebook - and it's because it's this very high-achieving area, and there's so much pressure to achieve at that level ... basically, if you're not striving to do something huge and earth-shaking, and if you're in fact just a teenager having struggles with grades, you feel like you've done something wrong, even when all you're doing is just trying to live your life. If you then have an underlying mental health disorder, it's doubly or triply difficult to maintain the level of artifice it requires.

I've been in therapy more or less my whole life - and I've definitely done a lot of therapy about grounding techniques and meditation - things that are meant to be centring and counter feelings of depersonalization. Mindfulness is a big thing people talk about, and I've found that my anxiety medication really helps. Mindfulness is hard because the last thing you want is to spend more time thinking about yourself when you're in those moments, but that is something I've spent a lot of time working through. I feel I rely too much on the meds sometimes.

Jenny

My first severe episode was, and still is, the most terrifying thing that has ever happened to me. I was lying on my bed when suddenly I felt as though my whole body had gone numb. My arms – from my elbows to my hands – felt limp, and my legs felt the same. It was the same feeling you get when you sleep on an arm and you wake up and all the blood has gone from it. When I looked at my arms and hands, they somehow looked as though they didn't belong to me. I could move them but it was as though I was controlling them through a computer screen. I was consumed by a feeling of dread so intense that I thought I was about to die.

This deadness in my arms was so 'real' that I felt I couldn't use my hands to make a phone call. Eventually, I managed to dial 999, and then my sister. Luckily, she lived close by and made her way over to my house. I later realized the symptoms may have been related to panic but I don't remember talking to anyone about it.

I remained very frightened for many months. I would regularly look down at my hands – for example, when I was using my phone – to find they suddenly looked as although they were not mine. I would also have anxious episodes where it would feel as though my 'soul' or 'spirit' or 'self' – whatever you'd refer to it as – would jump suddenly out of my body and hover above my head. This feeling would almost always be triggered by anxiety (e.g. when meeting new people). It was only when I saw a therapist who mentioned the word 'depersonalization' that I was able to Google the condition. It was such a relief to come across Jane's *Guardian* article [Swains 2015].

I continued to have episodes for a couple of years, but they grew less and less frequent. They were, however, accompanied by intensely dark existential feelings that I am still trying to come to terms with but which are fading with time. I am completely in awe of people who manage to live day-to-day with this condition. I would rather experience a panic attack every day than have to experience that dreadful feeling again. I wouldn't wish it on my worst enemy.

Heather

I wouldn't know I have DPD without the internet. I self-diagnosed, as it was clearly what I was experiencing. I have seen two psychologists in my life. The first one (in France) made a somewhat amused face when I mentioned having read about DPD online, and then proceeded with the therapy as if I hadn't mentioned it. The second (in the UK) has taken me more seriously but she doesn't know much about it. She did not, however, recognize the problem of the lack of awareness in the mental health community about DPD - she told me that in school they study all disorders and none of them particularly in depth, so it was normal that practitioners had scarce knowledge of it.

This is such an important aspect of DPD, not only in terms of diagnosis but also in terms of how you can experience it and communicate it - nobody knows [about] it; you have to explain it all, each and every time. And it's so hard to explain. The irony is precisely this: a disorder that makes you feel invisible is invisible in society; and a disorder that is so hard to explain has to be explained all the time. For me, DPD at times provokes a particularly disturbing thing: having a constant doubt about words. They sound weird - I doubt that what I just said made any sense, and I constantly think I have just made up words. How do you explain a disorder that makes you lose the sense of words? The lack of awareness just makes the feeling of detachment and loneliness and the impossibility to express myself worse.

Mara

In terms of what has worked so far – in a word: nothing. I did have a really odd experience once at work, which might be worth noting though. I don't think I was actually on medication at the time and I was in a really high-pressure conference in Seattle. I was about to do a presentation in front of the Vice President and a few others when I got a sudden flash of reality. It was almost as though the stress of the situation made me realize that I was actually there and about to do this very real thing, and I suddenly got a real sense of awareness – like a jolt. But my mind quickly shut it down as though to quell the fear. This really fits with the notion of the defence mechanism, so I think it is really interesting.

Meeting other sufferers and getting involved in the Unreal charity has really helped. I hadn't met anyone else with the condition until just over a year ago, so it was quite a major thing after all that time in the wilderness. I was worried that getting in too deep with helping others might compound the issue, but it's kind of had the opposite effect. I think it's a really good form of distraction and there's a real sense of camaraderie.

Michael

About Unreal

Unreal is the UK charity for Depersonalization and Derealization Disorder. Formally established in 2019, the charity's main aims are to reach out to people with lived experience of the condition and raise much-needed awareness. The board of volunteers includes people with lived experience, clinicians and carers – with leading neuropsychiatrist Professor Anthony David and singer–songwriter dodie as ambassadors.

The Unreal website contains information about the condition, details of current events – such as peer support sessions, live streams and third-party research studies – and details of how to get involved. Much of the charity's work is centred around signposting to appropriate resources and uniting people through the sharing of experiences.

For more information, please visit **www.unrealuk.org**
UK charity number: 1186498

Letter to My Friends (2017)

This is something I've felt I should write for a while.

As you probably already know, I've had some health struggles in my life for many years now. It's always been something difficult to talk about, but over time I've become more comfortable sharing my story rather than hiding it. In a strange way, it's only recently become necessary to be so open about my problems – mainly because of the situation it's leaving me in as I'm getting older.

As a teenager, anything goes – but when somebody is 27, largely unemployed and living back with his parents, it's easy to make assumptions. I've never been one to worry too much about people's opinions of me (look at the hair...) but I'd rather my close friends know the truth than be left wondering what's going on. So...

For around nine years I've had a psychological condition now believed to be depersonalization disorder (often abbreviated to DPD). It hasn't yet been officially diagnosed, but I've been referred to a psychiatric hospital in London called the Maudsley, which has the only clinic in the UK specializing in treating it. My referral has been accepted, but getting funding from the local commissioning group to send me is proving to be a nightmare. There's also a long waiting list for treatment, but when I finally do get there it's almost a certainty that the expected diagnosis will be given.

A brief history. My problems started when I was 18 and have progressively worsened over time – they're still getting worse now. Nobody can say for sure what brought them on, but it was most likely many years of bullying and emotional stress. They were also possibly triggered in 2008 by a one-off, strong dose of cannabis. Yes, we've probably all tried it. It's no big deal, right? Well...kind of. Cannabis wasn't something I'd really tried before, but one night five cookies were consumed. I'm not proud of it, but I can't deny doing it either.

It's believed that during times of particularly high stress or trauma, our brain tries to protect us from emotional pain by dissociating us from our sense of reality – it's a very normal reaction. But, if these stressful situations are particularly severe or go on for long periods of time, the brain can get to a point where it can't cope anymore and shuts down its emotional responses permanently – which is essentially DPD. For people who are already close to that point, cannabis can tip them over the edge.

The last nine years have in many ways been a process of elimination. I've seen (deep breath...) many GPs, neurologists, psychologists, psychiatrists, dieticians, hypnotherapists, endocrinologists, counsellors and therapists. I've had a brain MRI, an EEG, hundreds of blood tests, counselling, EMDR therapy, cognitive behavioural therapy, hypnotherapy, been on several exclusion diets, filled myself full of nutritional supplements, was sent on an anxiety course and briefly put on Prozac. So far, nothing has relieved the symptoms in any way.

It's almost impossible to explain how depersonalization feels, other than to say that life permanently feels like a dream. Nothing feels real. I struggle to feel all but the most extreme (and usually negative) emotions. I look in the mirror and it doesn't feel like myself I'm looking at. It's like I'm floating, not actually experiencing the world and slowly fading away into nothing. It's like I'm on autopilot in somebody else's body.

The best analogy I've found that most people can relate to is a sensation of feeling permanently drunk – just without slowed reactions. Imagine you're in a pub having consumed a lot of alcohol. You look around: it's noisy and busy, but you feel numbed and detached from it all. You see everything that's happening, but it seems unreal and you don't really internalize any of it. You talk to people seemingly without conscious thought about what you're saying – words just come out and they seem to make sense. The next day, it all feels like a hazy dream. The memories feel fake. It's almost like you're remembering a scene from a film, or a story that somebody told you about somebody else. It feels like you weren't actually there yourself.

That's what life is like for me every day, 24/7. Those feelings never go away. Life is a constant, exhausting mental battle to reassure myself that things aren't as entirely false as they feel.

Depersonalization is said to be one of the most distressing psychological problems you can have, because we're acutely aware that feeling this way is completely wrong. Although we all experience unreality occasionally, being trapped this way permanently is completely exhausting and debilitating.

Perhaps the most difficult aspect of having it is that to other people, there often appears to be nothing wrong. I can hold a conversation, drive a car, write music, etc. But how I might appear outwardly is absolutely the opposite to how I feel in my head. I've achieved a lot in the last nine years – and I still do, in some ways. But feeling as I do whilst somehow getting through each day and interacting with people without them noticing is something that makes no sense to me. Even my closest friends and family aren't aware of my struggles most of the time. It genuinely scares me how invisible this condition is to everybody but myself.

For the first six or so years, I could still do a lot of the things I wanted to do and live a fairly normal life, even though I was struggling internally. I survived university, worked several jobs and wrote a lot of music. But now, the depersonalization has become so bad that I cannot just pretend it doesn't exist anymore – it affects absolutely every aspect of my life. Even playing guitar can be a struggle now.

Some days I have to spend most of my time lying in bed. I have to concentrate so hard on basic tasks that I get bad headaches and have to rest. I can be very forgetful. I'm permanently exhausted. I sometimes muddle my words and have to slow my speech right down. I often stare off into the distance in a daze. I can be very quiet. I'm struggling so much now that I can't even begin to think about working another 9-to-5. I cannot move forward with my life or cope with much in the real world – and that makes me feel somewhat pathetic.

One of the things that upsets me most, though, is how the depersonalization has inevitably become my defining feature as an adult. Especially now that I've had to move back home, it's obvious to outsiders that something might be up – and it's something people ask about. It's nobody's fault – people are naturally curious – but it frustrates me that I can't be out living my life and doing much bigger and better things that would be far more interesting talking points for everyone. I hate feeling like I'm the awkward situation people tiptoe around, especially with family friends. The 'I'm a musician' line only gets you so far once people start digging.

For now, I'm fighting to get the necessary funding to get me to the Maudsley Hospital – NHS provisions for specialist mental health treatment are notoriously poor. It also seems I now have to get another local psychiatrist's report before I can apply for that funding. Once I do get there though, I genuinely believe the Maudsley will be able to help me. I genuinely believe that one day I will be able to feel things again, that the world around me will seem real again and I will finally be able to get on with everything I want to do in life after these years of being held back. It's mentally draining, but I do believe I will beat this illness.

If there's anything else you'd like to know about any of this, please don't be afraid to ask me – actually, talking about it helps. I should say, too, if you've been around me in the past and thought I've been disinterested or distant, or if I've been bad at staying in touch with you recently, I promise it's not because of you. Please just know that this is not the life I dreamed of when I was younger – and it's certainly not the life I dream of now.

Perky

References

Adlington, K., Hunter, E.C.M, David, A.S., Charlton, J. & Godlee, F. (2017) '"Watching the world through a clear fog" – recognising depersonalisation and derealization.' BMJ Talk Machine. Accessed 2 June 2020 at https://soundcloud.com/bmjpodcasts/watching-the-world-through-a-clear-fog-recognising-depersonalisation-and-derealisation.

AMA (2020) *ICD-1-VM 2020: The Complete Official Codebook*. Chicago, IL: American Medical Association (AMA).

APA (2013) *Diagnostic and Statistical Manual of Mental Disorders (5th edition; DSM-5)*. Washington, DC: American Psychological Association (APA) Publishing.

Baker, D., Hunter, E.C.M., Lawrence, E. & David, A.S. (2010) *Overcoming: Depersonalization and Feelings of Unreality*. London: Robinson.

Baker, D., Hunter, E.C.M., Lawrence, E., Medford, N. *et al.* (2003) 'Depersonalisation disorder: Clinical features of 204 cases.' *British Journal of Psychiatry* 182, 428–423.

Bezzubova, E. (2016) 'The "airbag" of depersonalization: Shield or disorder?' *Psychology Today*. Accessed 1 April 2020 at www.psychologytoday.com/gb/blog/the-search-self/201602/the-airbag-depersonalization-shield-or-disorder.

Bezzubova, E. (2018) 'Digital depersonalization: Losing self between reality and cyberspace.' *Psychology Today*. Accessed 21 June 2020 at www.psychologytoday.com/gb/blog/the-search-self/201801/digital-depersonalization.

Bezzubova, E. (2019) 'Marijuana–depersonalization controversies.' *Psychology Today*. Accessed 17 May 2020 at www.psychologytoday.com/gb/blog/the-search-self/201911/marijuana-depersonalization-controversies.

Bhandari, S. (2020) 'How common is dissociative identity disorder?' WebMD. Accessed 13 March 2020 at www.webmd.com/mental-health/qa/how-common-is-dissociative-identity-disorder.

Bird, J.C., Evans, R., Waite, F., Loe, B.S. & Freeman, D. (2018) 'Adolescent paranoia: Prevalence, structure, and casual mechanisms.' *Schizophrenia Bulletin 45*, 5, 1134–1142. Accessed 19 June 2020 at https://academic.oup.com/schizophreniabulletin/article/45/5/1134/5237786.

Boyle, F. (2020) *Prometheus Vol. 3*. Accessed 1 June 2020 at www.frankieboyle.com/prometheus-vol-3.

Burke, H. (2019) Quoted in 'How is technology overload affecting our physical and mental health?' *Icon*. Accessed 16 June 2020 at www.iconeye.com/design/features/technology-overload-mind-body-mental-health.

Campbell, A. (2019) *Alasdair Campbell: Depression and Me*. London: BBC. Accessed 2 June 2020 at www.bbc.co.uk/iplayer/episode/m0005btv/alastair-campbell-depression-and-me.

Černis, E., Freeman, D. & Ehlers, A. (2020) 'Describing the indescribable: A qualitative study of dissociative experiences in psychosis.' *PLoS 15*, 2, e0229091. Accessed 19 February 2020 at https://journals.plos.org/plosone/article?id=10.1371/journal.pone.0229091.

Charoensukmongkol, P. (2015) 'Mindful Facebooking: The moderating role of mindfulness on the relationship between social media use intensity at work and burnout.' *Journal of Health Psychology 21*, 9. DOI:10.1177/1359105315569096.

Ciaunica, A. & Charlton, J. (2018) 'When the self slips.' *Aeon*. Accessed 10 March 2020 at https://aeon.co/essays/what-can-depersonalisation-disorder-say-about-the-self.

Colizzi, M., Costa, R., Todarello, O. (2015) 'Dissociative symptoms in individuals with gender dysphoria: Is the elevated prevalence real?' *Psychiatry Research* 226, 1, 173–180.

David, A.S. (2020) *Into the Abyss*. London: Oneworld Publications.

Davis, N. (2019) 'High-strength cannabis increases risk of mental health problems.' *The Guardian*. Accessed 15 June 2020 at www.theguardian.com/society/2019/mar/19/high-strength-cannabis-increases-risk-of-mental-health-problems.

Dunne, N. (2019) '"I'm not me": A bizarre disorder leaves people feeling distant from their bodies.' *The Washington Post*. Accessed 28 May 2020 at www.washingtonpost.com/health/im-not-me-a-bizarre-disorder-leaves-people-feeling-distant-from-their-bodies/2019/06/28/aab4a75e-5d48-11e9-842d-7d3ed7eb3957_story.html.

Eddy, C.M. (2016) 'The junction between the self and other? Temporo-parietal dysfunction in neuropsychiatry.' University of Birmingham. Accessed 26 May 2020 at http://pure-oai.bham.ac.uk/ws/files/31183266/Eddy_junction_between_self_other_Neuropsychiatrica.pdf.

Gallup Jr., G.G. (1970) 'Chimpanzees: Self-recognition.' *Science* 167, 3914, 86–87.

Gresinger, W. (1845) *Die Pathologie und Therapie der Psychischen Krankheiten*. Stuttgart: Krabbe. (As referenced and quoted in M. Sierra (2009) *Depersonalization – A New Look at a Neglected Syndrome*. New York, NY: Cambridge University Press.)

Hari, J. (2018) *Lost Connections: Uncovering the Real Causes of Depression – and the Unexpected Solutions*. London: Bloomsbury.

Hari, J. (2019) *This Could Be Why You're Depressed or Anxious*. TED Talk, 11 October. Accessed 13 March 2020 at https://youtu.be/MB5IX-np5fE.

Headspace (nd) 'What is mindfulness?' Headspace. Accessed 20 June 2020 at www.headspace.com/mindfulness.

Healthline (2017) '13 signs and symptoms of Lyme disease.' Healthline. Accessed 2 June 2020 at www.healthline.com/health/lyme-disease-symptoms#cognitive-decline.

Healthline (2019) 'EMDR therapy: What you need to know.' Healthline. Accessed 4 May 2020 at www.healthline.com/health/emdr-therapy.

Hunter, E.C.M., Sierra, M. & David, A.S. (2004) 'The epidemiology of depersonalisation and derealisation.' *Social Psychiatry and Psychiatric Epidemiology 39*, 9–18. DOI:10.1007/s00127-004-0701-4.

Hunter, E.C.M., Salkovskis, P.M. & David, A.S. (2013) 'Attributions, appraisals and attention for symptoms in depersonalisation disorder.' *Behaviour Research and Therapy 53*, 20–29.

Hunter, E.C.M., Charlton, J. & David, A.S. (2017) 'Depersonalisation and derealisation: Assessment and management.' *British Medical Journal 356*, j745.

Jones, Z. (2018) 'Depersonalization in gender dysphoria: Widespread and widely unrecognized.' *Medium.* Accessed 13 March 2020 at https://medium.com/@zinniajones/depersonalization-in-gender-dysphoria-widespread-and-widely-unrecognized-baaac395bcb0.

Kleinman, Z. (2020) 'Half of UK 10-year-olds own a smartphone.' BBC. Accessed 16 June 2020 at www.bbc.co.uk/news/technology-51358192.

Knapton, S. (2018) 'Cyberbullying makes young people twice as likely to self harm or attempt suicide.' *The Telegraph.* Accessed 13 June 2020 at www.telegraph.co.uk/science/2018/04/22/cyberbullying-makes-young-people-twice-likely-self-harm-attempt.

Lawrence, U. (2015) 'Ute's story: Into the fog'. PTSD Association of Canada. Accessed 18 May 2020 at www.ptsdassociation.com/storiesb/2015/2/12/into-the-fog.

Loewenstein, R.J. (2018) 'Dr Richard J. Loewenstein talks about the misdiagnosis of dissociative disorders.' Austen Riggs Center. Accessed 21 June 2020 at https://vimeo.com/273538985.

Löken, L.S., Wessberg, J., Morrison, I., McGlone, F. & Olausson, H. (2009) 'Coding of pleasant touch by unmyelinated afferents in humans.' *Nature Neuroscience 12*, 547–548.

Maron, M. (2014) *Attempting Normal.* New York, NY: Spiegel & Grau.

McNamara, P. (2013) 'Sleep, dreams, and dissociation.' *Psychology Today*. Accessed 16 June 2020 at www.psychologytoday.com/gb/blog/dream-catcher/201311/sleep-dreams-and-dissociation.

Medford, N., Baker, D., Hunter, E.C.M., Sierra, M. *et al.* (2003) 'Chronic depersonalisation following illicit drug use: A controlled analysis of 40 cases.' *Addiction 98*, 12, 1731–1736.

Mind (2019) 'Dissociation and dissociative disorders.' Mind. Accessed 1 April 2020 at www.mind.org.uk/information-support/types-of-mental-health-problems/dissociation-and-dissociative-disorders/about-dissociation.

Morgan, E. (2016) *Anxiety for Beginners: A Personal Investigation*. London: Bluebird.

National Organization for Rare Disorders (2007) 'Depersonalization disorder.' National Organization for Rare Disorders. Accessed 20 January 2020 at https://rarediseases.org/rare-diseases/depersonalization-disorder.

Nelson, J. (2019) *Jesy Nelson: 'Odd One Out'*. BBC. Accessed 20 June 2020 at www.bbc.co.uk/iplayer/episode/p07lsr4d/jesy-nelson-odd-one-out.

NHS (2019) 'Overview: Schizophrenia.' Accessed 3 April 2020 at https://www.nhs.uk/conditions/schizophrenia.

NHS (2020) 'Overview: Gender dysphoria.' NHS. Accessed 13 March 2020 at https://www.nhs.uk/conditions/gender-dysphoria.

O'Brien, C. (2019) 'Mental health expert warns of "significant increase" in cannabis-induced psychosis.' CTV News. Accessed 15 June 2020 at www.ctvnews.ca/canada/mental-health-expert-warns-of-significant-increase-in-cannabis-induced-psychosis-1.4233512.

Pope, M. (2020) *Being Gail Porter*. BBC. Accessed 19 April 2020 at www.bbc.co.uk/iplayer/episode/m000df09/being-gail-porter.

Rhodes, J. (2016) *Music and the Inner Self*. TEDx Talks. Accessed 11 June 2020 at www.youtube.com/watch?v=QUUFb-1hBtw.

Savage, T. (2015) *Is Ambition Killing Us?* TEDx Talks. Accessed 27 May 2020 at https://youtu.be/FZBo1j5Zmbo.

Schabinger, N., Gillmeister, H., Berti, S., Michal, M., Beutel, M.E. & Adler, J. (2018) 'Detached and distracted: ERP correlates of altered attentional function in depersonalisation.' *Biological Psychology 134*, 64–71.

Schauer, M. & Elbert, T. (2010) 'Dissociation following traumatic stress.' *Zeitschrift für Psychologie 218*, 2. DOI:10.1027/0044-3409/a000018. Accessed 19 June 2020 at www.researchgate.net/publication/230651567_Dissociation_Following_Traumatic_Stress.

Sierra, M. (2009) *Depersonalization – A New Look at a Neglected Syndrome.* New York, NY: Cambridge University Press.

Simeon, D. (2004) 'Depersonalisation disorder: A contemporary overview.' *CNS Drugs 18*, 343–354.

Simeon, D. & Abugel, J. (2006) *Feeling Unreal: Depersonalization Disorder and the Loss of the Self.* New York, NY: Oxford University Press

Simeon, D., Gross, S., Guralnik, O., Stein, D.J., Schmeidler, J. & Hollander, M.D. (1997) 'Feeling unreal: 30 cases of DSM-III-R depersonalization disorder.' *The American Journal of Psychiatry 154*, 8, 1107– 1113.

Simeon, D., Knutelska, M., Nelson, D. & Guralnik, O. (2003) 'Feeling unreal: A depersonalization disorder update of 117 cases.' *Journal of Clinical Psychiatry 64*, 9, 990–7. Accessed 12 April 2020 at www.ncbi.nlm.nih.gov/pubmed/14628973.

Smart TMS (nd) 'TMS and DPD – the evidence.' Smart TMS. Accessed 5 May 2020 at www.smarttms.co.uk/depersonalisation-disorder/tms-results-evidence.

Swains, H. (2015) 'Depersonalisation disorder: The condition you've never heard of that affects millions.' *The Guardian*, 4 September. Accessed 11 January 2020 at www.theguardian.com/society/2015/sep/04/depersonalisation-disorder-the-condition-youve-never-heard-of-that-affects-millions.

Teller, R.J. (2017) *Teller Explains Why He Remains Silent on Stage.* User Four. Accessed 23 April 2020 at https://youtu.be/YJRIkTHqTSE.

Thomson, P. & Jaque, S.V. (2020) 'Multifaceted self-consciousness: Depersonalization, shame, flow, and creativity in performing artists.' *Psychology of Consciousness: Theory, Research, and Practice.* DOI: 10.1037/cns0000228.

Tracey, K. (2017) '"It's quite freaky, like something's prodding my brain."' BBC. Accessed 29 May 2020 at www.bbc.co.uk/news/health-40705512.

Van Der Kolk, B. (2014) *The Body Keeps The Score: Mind, Brain and Body in the Transformation of Trauma.* London: Penguin Random House.

Watts, R. (2017) *Can Magic Mushrooms Unlock Depression?* TEDx Talks. Accessed 27 May 2020 at www.youtube.com/watch?v=8kfGaVAXeMY.